XL

Allan Sefton ... .
a lot of travelling. This provided opportunities ... ...e's
passion for fishing. He has successfully chased many species of fish
from the Falkland Islands via equatorial Pacific Islands to the Arctic
Circle. But his favourite fish are Atlantic salmon and his favoured destination is Scotland.

Retirement from his first career meant a chance to qualify as a Level
Two Game Angling Coach. He gets great pleasure from introducing
others to the joys of fly fishing and has worked with others to coach
and encourage the Angling Trust's Team England Youth Fly Fishing.
He also became a regular contributor to *Trout and Salmon*, the UK's
premier game fishing magazine.

Allan lives in Cambridgeshire near Grafham Water and other res-
ervoirs that boast some of the finest 'big water' trout fly fishing in
Europe. But this does not stop him spending several weeks each year
in pursuit of salmon. This is his second book.

FLY FISHING FOR SALMON

Allan Sefton

A How To Book

ROBINSON

ROBINSON

First published in Great Britain in 2015 by Robinson

A CIP catalogue record for this book
is available from the British Library.

ISBN: 978-1-47213-562-9 (paperback)
ISBN: 978-1-47213-563-6 (ebook)

Typeset by TW Typesetting, Plymouth, Devon
Printed and bound by CPI Group (UK) Ltd, Croydon, CR0 4YY

Robinson
is an imprint of
Little, Brown Book Group
Carmelite House
50 Victoria Embankment
London EC4Y 0DZ

An Hachette UK Company

www.hachette.co.uk
www.littlebrown.com

How To Books are published by Robinson, an imprint of Little, Brown Book
Group. We welcome proposals from authors who have first-hand experience
of their subjects. Please set out the aims of your book, its target market and its
suggested contents in an email to Nikki.Read@howtobooks.co.uk

CONTENTS

ACKNOWLEDGEMENTS

Dr Sean Tighe, Dr Chris Dobbs and John Veitch helped by providing essential information on distant destinations.

Thanks also to my wife, Jenn, who has coped cheerfully with many holidays on the banks of salmon rivers.

ILLUSTRATIONS

FOREWORD

There are few moments in life that one will truly never forget, but I am certain that among them for me will be the moment when I hooked and landed my first salmon. I have re-played it in my mind on countless occasions since: the urgent tug on the line, the thrashing of a great tail that stirred up a boiling froth of peaty white water, the wailing of my reel as the fish headed off downstream at speed and the overwhelming relief as at last it slipped into my landing net. The take of a salmon is a moment of pure magic that makes even those anglers who are lucky and persistent enough to have caught thousands of fish in their lives keep coming back for more.

If you are new to salmon fishing, this book by Allan Sefton is an excellent source of information to help you get started, and it also provides a very good summary of the biology, geography and politics surrounding this magnificent fish. With the privilege of fishing for salmon comes a responsibility to understand how precious and threatened these fish are, and how we as anglers can help protect them now and in the future.

Over the past century, we have sucked rivers dry; smothered spawning gravels with soil; polluted waters with pesticides, fertilisers and sewage; blocked rivers with dams, weirs and hydropower turbines; infested coastal waters with sea lice from salmon farms and netted vast quantities of fish at sea. Considering what humans have done to salmon, it's remarkable that we have any left at all! In many rivers stocks are dangerously low. Dr Ronald Campbell, who led the restoration of Tweed salmon stocks, makes the point that fisheries management is not about managing fish, it's about managing people. These fish are highly adaptable and have a powerful survival instinct; all we need to do is stop people from polluting, abstracting, damming and netting.

Anglers are an important part of the solution too. We are getting much better at putting fish back, and putting them back carefully, rather than killing everything we catch as people did in the past. We invest far more money and volunteer time than any other group to support the excellent work of the Rivers and Fisheries Trusts. Anglers represent a big political constituency, and tens of thousands of anglers have joined the Angling Trust to support its work campaigning for fish and fishing, which is united with Fish Legal's work using the law to protect fish stocks and the rights of its members throughout the UK.

There is, famously, more to fishing than catching fish. Salmon live in some of the most beautiful places in the world and I hope that you enjoy those places to the full while you wait for that unmistakable tug on the end of the line . . .

Mark Lloyd
CEO, Angling Trust and Fish Legal

INTRODUCTION

Salmon fly fishing is a surprisingly modern sport. It is the latest chapter in our relationship with the world's most iconic fish.

In Europe modern salmon fly fishing was triggered by a decline in salmon catches that has revolutionised the economics of Scottish salmon angling over the last thirty years.

Even the aristocratic, conservative old guard that had dominated Scottish salmon angling were not prepared to tolerate catching no, or few, salmon year after year. And they had other places to go. Alaska was becoming ever more accessible and success was predictable. Iceland was bucking the trend of lower catches and pitching for the luxury market. And a whole new Atlantic salmon universe was opening up on the Kola Peninsula in north-western Russia. It was a bit primitive, perhaps, and the travel arrangements could be challenging, but the salmon numbers and catches enjoyed by the pioneers made it all worthwhile. They still do.

Not surprisingly, many owners of Scottish salmon fishing rights began to bail out too. Beats were 'timeshared' to anglers who bought a specific week each season in perpetuity or sold to 'new money' from the City or overseas investors looking to buy into the dream of owning a Scottish sporting estate.

The result has been the opening of Scottish salmon fishing to ordinary anglers who had long been excluded by the 'closed shop' as much as the price. This availability is a trend that continues to accelerate. The Internet age means that even those of modest means can find a day on a 'top beat' at the click of a mouse. Prime weeks may still be very expensive, and are booked well in advance, but they are available.

The comparative shortage of salmon also changed attitudes.

In the past, every rod-caught salmon had been killed. The aim was always to maximise 'the bag' and any method was employed. Slowly it dawned that declining catches could, in part, be the result of killing the goose that laid the golden egg.

Fishers returned from Alaska and Russia where 'catch-and-release' were practised and asked why Scotland should be different. Today most Scottish salmon caught on rod and line are released.

How salmon were caught also became more important than how many. Beats became 'fly-only' as a salute to an increasingly precious resource. It was an approach that said, 'If salmon are scarce, let's catch them in the most skilful and elegant manner'. Surprisingly, perhaps, this did not become an impediment to catching them. Instead, it brought about a welcome, rapid and continuing improvement in salmon fly fishing technology. Today, the rods, lines and other means of presenting a salmon fly at the desired depth in a difficult stream are incomparably better than they were twenty years ago.

It is ironic that the two most famous, and most loved, salmon fishing books published during the latter half of the twentieth century, *Salmon* by Arthur Oglesby, first published by Macdonald and Janes in 1971 and *Salmon Fishing* by Hugh Falkus, first published by H.F. and G.Witherby Ltd in 1984 both described good times that were already fading. Of course, much of the excellent, practical advice they contain is timeless, but they missed the development of the tackle and the approaches that make salmon fly fishing so satisfying and exciting today.

The purpose of this book is to fill this gap.

Fly Fishing for Salmon provides concise, practical advice on modern fly fishing and on the latest techniques and tackle. It aims to transform aspiration into achievement whether you are an absolute beginner keen to hook a first salmon or an old hand planning to catch even more salmon around the world.

Finally, *Fly Fishing for Salmon* is perfect for those fly fishers who need little help for themselves but are eager to introduce their spouses, children or grandchildren to a great fishing experience.

ONE

A BRIEF HISTORY

Salmon are a northern fish. They are most at home in the northern oceans and the cold, infertile, fast-flowing rivers of north-west Europe, Alaska, Russia and Canada. They prosper north of the Arctic Circle. They can even breed in rivers that are ice-bound for eight months of the year. They migrate for thousands of kilometres to feed among the icebergs in the world's coldest seas.

Just imagine the impact of salmon on the lives of our distant ancestors. Adventurous hunter-gatherers, who forged their way north in search of game, found rivers that supported only a limited population of small resident fish. Then suddenly, every summer, shoals of a huge, silver, marine fish ran to the headwaters of these streams to lay their eggs. Their size was out of all proportion to the river's shallow water, fast currents and uncertain volumes. The salmon were highly visible and easily caught by humans, bears or eagles. They provided a source of (delicious!) protein that could sustain their populations through the long winter to come.

They still do. Today this wonderful natural resource is embedded in our culture as the king of fish.

SALMON FISHING RIGHTS

As is the way of the world, 'ownership' and the rights to fish for and to protect the salmon soon became vexing issues. In Great Britain some of the earliest parliamentary legislation ensured that the aristocracy and wealthy landowners reaped the bounty from the rivers and shores of their estates. The sale of game, including salmon, was a significant source of income to them at a time when all meat and fish was difficult to rear, harvest and transport.

Later, when the industrial revolution provided new, undreamed-of sources of wealth, many salmon streams in England and parts of Scotland were sacrificed to provide sources of power or drains for toxic effluents. The new railways also provided the means to transport highly perishable fish of all species to cities and towns to meet an ever-growing demand.

The salmon became a fish under pressure. Although already a luxury, its value increased. So did the strength of the laws to reinforce landowners' ownership of fisheries and to prevent illegal fishing.

In the New World, where many had emigrated to escape the tyranny of wealthy landowners and overcrowded cities, a different, unregulated, approach followed the 'discovery' of prolific salmon fisheries, particularly in Alaska. Enterprising individuals established commercial fisheries and canneries on river banks and profited massively. They processed all the fish they could catch and eventually sold small cans of salmon as a luxury food to a worldwide market.

Bust inevitably followed this bonanza. More and more companies tried to cash in, and even the most prolific wild salmon populations could not withstand this assault. Federal and state controls followed, not to monopolise ownership or to prevent citizens from fishing, but to limit catches. The aim was to manage the fishery to ensure sustainable populations. There could then be an annual harvest, shared equitably, as the stocks of fish moved inshore to run into their natal rivers to breed.

Today, the Alaska Fish and Game Department's management of salmon is the world's best example of how to protect and enhance stocks of wild salmon. Commercial fishing prospers, their catch is sold around the world and huge numbers of anglers converge on the state each summer. The enthusiasm of the sport fishers, and the salmon-filled rivers they find, have created good business for the fishing lodges, and much-needed employment for guides, plane operators and all the state's associated tourist businesses.

Today, Alaska is the world's most accessible and most prolific salmon angling destination.

A VICTORIAN REVOLUTION

In Europe, the development of sport fishing for Atlantic Salmon followed a different path. The roots are in Scotland. When Queen Victoria ascended the throne of Great Britain early in the nineteenth century, Scotland was a long way from London. It was not an unpopulated wilderness, but it probably felt as isolated and unloved as some far-flung corners of the growing British Empire. Scotland's forests, its obvious natural resource, had already been cut down. The Highlands were a world apart from the capital, Edinburgh, the financial centre, and the trading ports of Glasgow and Dundee. Infertile soils provided meagre returns for peasant farming tenants and for their landlords.

Three economic events brought about a cultural revolution. Firstly, the landowners discovered that sheep, which could roam freely over the hills, were a better income source than tenant farmers. The infamous Highland Clearances began. This led to the flowering of Caledonian Societies across the New World and beyond as thousands of Scots who lived along Scotland's river banks were effectively expelled from their native land.

Secondly, Queen Victoria and her consort, Prince Albert, 'discovered' Scotland and fell in love with the Highlands. They built a castle at Balmoral on the banks of the Aberdeenshire Dee, one of Scotland's premier salmon rivers. They transformed their new estate into a sporting paradise. They spent the summer and early autumn there. They shot grouse, stalked deer and went fishing for fun. Soon, anyone who was anyone in the British Empire owned or rented a Highland estate. New castles sprang up. For the aristocracy, the *uber*-wealthy and the growing middle classes who emulated the royal family, it became *de rigueur* to enjoy a sporting holiday in Scotland each summer.

They were able to get there in some luxury because of a third economic miracle, the railways. Wealthy London families could hire a whole train for their friends and their retinue of servants. They would all leave a great London terminus such as Euston or King's Cross in the evening and wake up in a private Highland station the following morning. It was a journey that a generation earlier would have taken an uncomfortable week by sea or stagecoach.

Thus, it became more fashionable, and more profitable for some, to catch a salmon on rod and line than it did to sweep them out with nets.

These 'new' sporting traditions survived into the second half of the twentieth century. For all this time salmon fishing in both Scotland and England remained mostly a preserve of the very wealthy. There was some public fishing, and some local associations sprang up, but most salmon fishing 'beats' were rented by the week or longer. The same parties would take the same tenancy each year for family and friends. Even if you could afford it, turnover was slow and vacancies were scarce. It could take many years to fill 'dead men's shoes'.

THE FIRST ANGLING TOURISTS

In the first half of the twentieth century, many of the richest and most enthusiastic salmon fishers began to explore beyond Scotland. They started to travel to Norway and Iceland in the summer months. They were the first angling tourists. In Norway, landowners netted salmon but could be persuaded to rent their rights to rod fishers. The salmon they caught were bigger than most Scottish fish. Today there are still giant salmon caught each year in Norway, but they are hard won.

Iceland was also a long boat trip away and had a wide variety of rivers, many with prolific salmon runs. Nothing has changed, except that an enlightened Icelandic government has recognised that sport fishing for salmon brings more benefits than commercial fishing. Today salmon are only caught on rod and line in Iceland, mostly by fly fishing. Salmon fishing in Iceland was a costly adventure for those early travellers. That has not changed!

THE EVOLUTION OF FLY FISHING

During the second half of the twentieth century, Scottish salmon fishing enjoyed an ever-accelerating pace of change.

Before the 1980s, most Scottish salmon were caught by anglers who used spinners or bait. Spring and early summer were the cream of the season when the water was often high and cold. Even before fixed spool or multiplying reels were available, the use of spinners or heavy spoons was the easiest way to cast a long way and to get the lure well down in the water. Catching a salmon was more important than how you did it.

Fly fishing for salmon had always been a rather specialised technique. The original greenheart, spliced, double-handed rods commonly used in Scotland were heavy. They did not become much lighter when companies like Hardy of Alnwick introduced built-cane rods with metal ferrules. It took stamina to fish all day! The plaited silk fly lines demanded a lot of care and attention. Fashion demanded the use of fancy, intricate, expensive flies.

None of this deterred an enthusiastic band of fly fishing devotees! They were encouraged by the success of the innovative A.H.E. Wood, who rented the Cairnton beat of the River Dee for many years from 1903, and by a classic angling book, *Greased line fishing for Salmon*, which described his techniques, written by Jock Scott in 1939.

FROM FEAST TO FAMINE

The factor that brought about profound change was the salmon themselves. In the years following the Second World War, runs of salmon in Scotland were consistently good year after year. Historically, salmon runs in Great Britain were cyclical, with the populations in the major rivers changing over periods of fifty years or more. They swung between years when spring-run fish dominated catches to spells when the majority of the salmon ran in the early autumn. The 1960s and 70s were particularly good because, unusually, there were good runs in both spring and autumn.

On the minor Scottish rivers on the west coast of the Highlands and on the islands where, in midsummer, smaller salmon known as grilse, which had spent only one winter at sea, were the dominant runs, catches were also exceptional. Scientific research at the time showed remarkable at-sea survival rates of juvenile salmon. In some years, more than fifty per cent of the juveniles that migrated to sea from Scottish rivers returned as mature adults one or two years later.

It was too good to last. In the late 1970s and into the 80s, a decline set in. Part of the problem may have been a disease, Ulcerative Dermal Necrosis (UDN), which decimated the population in some rivers when it spread like wildfire through overcrowded pools, but it was not the whole problem. Over the last twenty years, the at-sea survival rates of juvenile salmon leaving European rivers have plummeted. It is now estimated that fewer than five per cent of the juvenile salmon that leave river estuaries return as adults. No one can explain this.

It is fortunate that during the same period in-river population densities of juvenile salmon have improved due to habitat improvement. And marine commercial fishing for salmon, which was originally feared to be the cause of the crisis, has almost ceased.

THE FUTURE

Currently, there is a new sense of optimism. Runs of Scottish salmon have increased since 2005, but this improvement has not been consistent. There were big increases in some years (2007 and 2010 were outstanding), but there has been a fall back since. 2014 has been dreadful. On some Scottish rivers catches were only half the five-year average. 2015 is much better so far. Overall, any recovery in Scottish salmon catches is fragile.

There are also specific pollution problems on the west coast of Scotland and the offshore islands and in parts of Norway, caused by fatal, parasitic 'sea-louse' infestations, which are a direct result of farming salmon in open-sea cages in lochs and bays through which juvenile wild salmon and sea trout have to run on their migration. This problem, like all pollution problems, is soluble, and there are signs that the people of Scotland are joining environmentalists in condemning the powerful salmon farming industry and their supine government and regulators. Nearly all salmon caught by anglers in Scotland are returned alive.

Today, partly due to the changes in Scotland, the world of salmon fishing is very different. Fly fishing for salmon is the method of choice. Huge developments have been made in modernising fly fishing tackle and techniques.

New salmon fishing destinations, such as the Kola Peninsula in Russia, have opened up, and new rivers and lodges are becoming available in Alaska and Iceland as money pours into new developments.

Salmon fly fishing may not yet be a sport for all, but it is opening up to many who thought it was beyond their means. It will always be a great privilege. Go and enjoy it!

TWO
SALMON SPECIES, RUNS AND SEASONS

The salmon is the king of fish for economic rather than sporting reasons. Hundreds of years ago, monks were the only inhabitants of Western Siberia. Perhaps they built their monasteries on that frozen land in order to pray and meditate, but they became wealthy by damming the rivers to harvest prolific salmon runs. Merchant ships from Holland and the Low Countries made the hazardous journey north each summer to buy their catch.

In the northern Pacific, native peoples survived the dark, cold winters by smoking, air-drying and freezing the salmon that ran in millions up their rivers. They still do today.

In Scotland, large estates whose lands were mostly unfertile mountain soil and bogs were enriched by netting the annual runs of salmon that arrived at the mouths of otherwise unproductive rivers.

Only recently has the wild salmon's sporting value been recognised. Today, many salmon populations are under threat. It is a depressing thought that as they become fewer and more difficult to find, their economic value as a sporting trophy will rise again.

PACIFIC SALMON

There are five species of Pacific Salmon that breed in the rivers that flow into the northern Pacific in Alaska, NW Canada, the USA, Russia and Asia. These fish support thriving commercial and sporting fisheries in Alaska, other Pacific Northwest states and Western Canada.

They are the Chinook (or King), the Coho (or silver), the Pink (or Humpy), the Sockeye (or Red) and the Chum (or Dog). These species are not equally rated by sports fishers.

The Chinook are the world's biggest salmon. 13 to 18 kg specimens are regularly caught. A burnished silver, black-spotted giant is a much-sought-after prize.

Smaller Coho Salmon, usually 2.7 to 5.4 kg, are even more beautiful. A fish fresh from the sea looks as if it has been newly dipped in molten silver. They fight tenaciously when hooked, leaping often in an effort to shed a hook. They are the favourite quarry of many of the fly fishers who visit Alaska. 'Kings' and 'Silvers' are not available everywhere, and if you are travelling to Alaska or elsewhere in the region, you have homework to do if you want to have a good chance of catching them. Like all salmon, their beauty fades, to human eyes, as they mature and get ready to spawn, but both species change less as they mature than the other Pacific species. This may explain their popularity with anglers.

The Sockeye Salmon is the most valuable commercially, and stocks have come under pressure. Fresh from the sea, they are as silver as a newly minted coin, but they quickly turn bright red on their body and olive green on the head. They usually weigh between 2.2 to 3 kg.

Chum Salmon have always been less popular with anglers because they have less culinary value, and they are not fished commercially (i.e. only suitable to feed dogs!). This is probably the reason there are huge runs on many rivers.

Unsurprisingly, anglers are catching on that this salmon, which can reach over 13 kg but is usually in the 3.6 to 8 kg range, takes flies and fights as hard as any other. It is a worthy quarry. Their prodigious numbers make it accessible to fly fishers who do not have the time or the means to chase the great Chinook or elusive Coho.

The smallest Pacific Salmon is the Pink, which averages only 1.3 to 2.3 kg. They have large black oval blotches on their backs and much smaller scales than the other species. They are silver and 'salmon-shaped' when fresh from the sea, but the males develop a prominent hump in front of their dorsal fin as they develop, hence their nickname: 'Humpy'. They fight strongly for their size and take a fly readily (see Figure 1).

All Pacific Salmon species die after spawning. Scientists believe that the nutrients and minerals derived from their rotting corpses enhance the fertility of the tundra and forests and, in turn, increase rivers' capacity to support subsequent populations of baby salmon.

The Pacific Salmon species migrate into the rivers at different times during the short Arctic summer. Their runs overlap, so late July to August would give you the greatest choice, but if your heart's desire is to catch a fresh, chrome-flanked Chinook, you should fish between late May and early July when these giants first enter fresh water. Sockeyes run from June to late July. Pinks and Chum Salmon peak between mid-July and mid-August. Coho salmon are later and have a slightly longer season, between July and October. There are variations across the region. Do your homework before you choose when and where to go.

ATLANTIC SALMON

There is only one species of Atlantic Salmon (*Salmo salar*). The species has a wide range. It breeds in rivers all around the North Atlantic including north-eastern Canada, Iceland and, on the eastern sea-board, from Siberia, Finland and northern Norway to Spain in the south.

Like all salmon, the fish return from the Atlantic to their native rivers to spawn. This means that thousands of distinct populations exist, and the different timings of the runs of spawning fish into individual rivers reflect this genetic integrity and the local environmental pressures.

In the north, the summer season is short as rivers can be ice-bound for six to seven months each year and runs of fish occur from June to September, which is when fishing takes place. Further south, where rivers are ice free, runs are spread through the year, but different patterns occur even on neighbouring rivers.

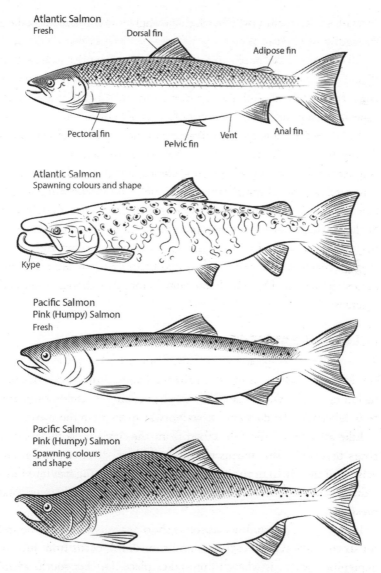

Atlantic Salmon
Fresh

Dorsal fin

Adipose fin

Pectoral fin

Pelvic fin

Vent

Anal fin

Atlantic Salmon
Spawning colours and shape

Kype

Pacific Salmon
Pink (Humpy) Salmon
Fresh

Pacific Salmon
Pink (Humpy) Salmon
Spawning colours
and shape

Fig. 1 – Atlantic salmon – a 'fresh' fish and one in breeding colour. Pacific salmon – the Pink or Humpy salmon – a fresh fish and one in breeding colour showing characteristic hump. This is one of the five species of Pacific Salmon.

Atlantic Salmon populations also exhibit significant local variations in the ages at which they mature and return to their natal rivers to spawn.

All Atlantic Salmon spawn by laying their eggs in nests known as 'redds' dug into gravel each autumn. Fry hatch out in spring to take advantage of increasing populations of plankton-like food. Young salmon or 'parr' live in the river for one or two years before, each May, they 'smolt' and acquire a distinctive silvery coat. They then make their way to the sea and begin their long migrations across the North Atlantic.

Currently, the difficult transition from fresh water to a life at sea claims the lives of many young Atlantic Salmon smolts. Scientists are struggling to fathom out why. Those that make it, grow quickly on a rich marine diet.

Most rivers have distinct runs of salmon that return to breed either as 'one sea-winter' (1SW) fish, 'two sea-winter fish' (2SW) or, rarely, as 'multi sea-winter' (MSW) fish.

GRILSE AND 'SPRINGERS'

One sea-winter fish are known as 'grilse'. The grilse in most rivers run from late July into autumn. They are beautiful small silver fish that usually weigh between 1.3 and 2.3 kg. In some rivers, such as Scotland's River Tweed, many grilse stay at sea longer and may not run until October. They weigh a kilogram or two more but are still grilse that have spent only one full winter at sea.

British and Irish salmon that do spend two winters at sea may return early in the year, between February and May, to the river of their birth. These are spring salmon or 'springers'. Both the fish and their rivers are greatly prized. These 'fresh' salmon, which weigh between 3.6 and 4.5 kg, enter rivers that are still cold; they usually travel only slowly upstream and can be eager to take a well-presented fly. They are gorgeous fish with pure-white bellies, gun-metal flanks and lilac-coloured backs. The cold water seems to preserve this coloration for many weeks, in contrast to salmon which run later in the year and rapidly acquire their duller, breeding hues (see Figure 1).

The most famous 'Spring Rivers' in Scotland are the Helmsdale and Aberdeenshire's Dee, but there are improving spring runs on the Tay, the Tweed and some northern highland rivers too.

On most other rivers, including those in Canada, Iceland, Norway and Russia, salmon runs of both 2SW salmon and grilse do not start before June and are petering out by the end of September.

There are lots of local variations. Years ago, the rivers on the west coast of Scotland and the Hebrides were essentially 'grilse-only' rivers. Today, these rivers are seeing better runs of 2SW fish. Their grilse runs are reducing and occurring later in the year. Similarly, some rivers in England and Wales that used to have good spring runs rarely see a spring fish today but have respectable numbers of grilse and 2SW fish in the late summer or autumn when the weather cools and the river levels rise.

No one knows why these changes occur. Some scientists believe that there may be natural selection of young salmon that smolt after only one year of river life in those rivers where the life of baby fish is most precarious. The salmon's life cycle is fragile. Young fish are at risk from flood, drought, frost, starvation and other hazards. Perhaps a one-year river life reduces the risk of a catastrophic event wiping out several-year classes. The evidence shows that these fish tend to return as grilse, while those parr that spend longer in the river return as 2SW adults. This may explain why small, rapid, perhaps inhospitable, streams tend to be grilse rivers while big, more productive, rivers like Scotland's Tay and Tweed produce runs of bigger salmon.

Grilse predominate in most rivers in Iceland but there are some, usually bigger, rivers with substantial runs of 2SW salmon.

RUSSIA AND 'OSENKA' SALMON

Most rivers on Russia's Kola Peninsula, such as the Yokanga, enjoy runs of 2SW fish with a good number of even bigger MSW salmon, including almost weekly catches of 30 kg-plus monsters. One river, the Ponoi, is famous for huge runs of grilse in July and August, which give mind-boggling catches of fifty fish per rod during a week's visit most years. Overall, salmon numbers on the well-managed rivers of the Kola peninsula are either stable or increasing.

Many of the Russian rivers also have a unique run of a class of Atlantic Salmon known as 'Osenka' fish. These fish, usually in the teens of kilograms and above and probably MSW fish, run into the rivers from late August until the cold weather begins to close in at the end of September. They are bright, muscular fish that survive the winter under the ice that covers the river from October, and they will not breed for another year. No one knows why these salmon do this. It may be safer for them to lie moribund under the tundra's ice than to spend the dark winter in the Barents Sea. Many salmon fishers believe this class of fish provides the cream of Russian salmon fishing, and they return each year to cast their flies at them. These fish also provide immediate sport in the spring of the following year when the ice breaks up and the first fishers arrive to greet the new season.

NORWAY AND BIG ATLANTIC SALMON

About ninety per cent of all Atlantic Salmon die after spawning, but a small number do survive, make it back to the sea and recover to grow bigger before returning to spawn for a second time. These MSW salmon can become the giant Atlantic Salmon that all salmon anglers dream of hooking. Anyone who has read Fred Buller's scholarly tome, *The Doomsday Book of Giant Salmon*, knows that giant salmon over 18 kg in weight are not old fish. Salmon just put on weight prodigiously the bigger they get, so a big, post-spawning fish that gets back to sea, or one that decides to stay at sea for three or four years before returning to the river, becomes very big indeed.

Buller's book tells us that Norway has always been a giant salmon destination, and that the Alta, a river in the far north of the country, was the best river of all for monsters. Norway, and the Alta, remains a giant fish mecca even if, inevitably, not as good as the glory days a century ago.

CANADA

Another rich source of giant salmon was the legendary Grand Cascapedia River in New Brunswick, Eastern Canada. This river is still a fabled and productive salmon producer, but, like so many eastern seaboard Canadian rivers, the glory days have passed. There is nowhere where Atlantic Salmon numbers have plummeted more than in some rivers in eastern Canada. No one knows why, despite considerable investment in salmon conservation and much scientific investigation. The situation is not hopeless. Some of the famous 'destination' rivers still attract dedicated salmon fly fishers, mostly from the USA. In Newfoundland and Labrador, some rivers still have good runs of grilse but, overall, eastern Canada highlights the Atlantic Salmon's fragile lifecycle. No nation with salmon stocks can be complacent.

LOCAL SALMON RUNS AND POPULATION CYCLES

In the UK, long-term accurate records of salmon numbers in different rivers show that salmon numbers have never been constant and that the timing of annual runs changes.

For example, on the River Tweed, Scotland's most prolific river, the timing of runs over the past 150 years follows a fifty-year cycle. Today, the biggest runs of salmon, both grilse and 2SW fish, take place in the autumn. October is the best month, but fresh fish enter the river right up to the end of November when the season closes. There is also a smaller, but improving, spring run on the Tweed between February and May. This is a 'new' run which is attracting anglers. Only a few years ago there was almost no spring run and the river was hardly fished.

Fifty years ago the spring run was the dominant run and very few fish ran in autumn. One hundred years ago this situation was reversed. Scientists (and fishers!) are wondering if today's improving spring runs are the first sign of another turn in the cycle and whether the spring will become dominant again soon.

What triggers this cycle? Will it be repeated? No one knows.

ANNUAL SALMON CATCH RETURNS IN SCOTLAND

The national records of rod and net catches of salmon in Scotland in the period 2007 to 2012 gave cause for optimism. Numbers seemed to be increasing and on some rivers catches were the best for thirty years. Anglers were returning alive nearly all the salmon they caught and in-river breeding populations were healthy. Re-stocking programmes carried out by some local fishery boards were ended, partly to follow a fashion for protecting 'genetic integrity'. This welcome recovery in adult salmon stocks stalled in 2013, and catches have plummeted further in 2014. No one knows why. The Scottish government has ordered a review into salmon population management in the country.

BUYER BEWARE!

The purpose of this chapter is to emphasise that the pursuit of wild salmon is a challenging game. It is not like popping down to the local club for a game of golf. It rewards research, planning and effort, but remains unpredictable.

The best salmon fishing in the world in Alaska, Russia and Iceland is more constant than most, and comes at considerable cost, but cannot be guaranteed.

The best advice is to act like a shrewd financial investor: 'get into a trend late and get out of a trend early'. And revel in success.

SUMMARY

◆ The five species of Pacific Salmon run at different times through the summer; time your trip accordingly.

◆ Do not ignore Chum Salmon. They are a good size, take flies and fight well.

◆ Atlantic Salmon are a single species, but the population from each river has unique characteristics. Research the timing of their runs.

◆ In the UK only a few rivers have 'spring runs' of salmon. Autumn runs dominate in most rivers.

◆ There is some evidence that the timing and nature of some Atlantic Salmon runs may be changing. Be alert for trends before planning a trip.

THREE
SALMON BEHAVIOUR

A fly fisher trying to attract a trout studies the insects or other invertebrates that trout eat. Anticipation of seasonal hatches and the response of the fish are a multi-layered puzzle. New imitative flies, and better 'presentation' to mimic the trout's prey, are at the heart of fly fishing.

Trout and other fish take 'lures' that do not imitate anything that swims. Fly fishers assume this is an instinctive reaction by an inquisitive and hungry predator.

Salmon, however, cannot digest food in fresh water and their stomachs are always empty. It is therefore a mystery why any salmon ever takes an artificial fly.

Most do not. But, at times, in certain places and for reasons not understood, one does. No one knows what makes this particular fish, perhaps one out of many swimming together, 'vulnerable'. The salmon does not eat, so the puzzle is not solved by studying prey and devising an even better imitation.

The salmon fly fisher has two overlapping options. The first is simply to fish long and hard. Keeping your fly in the water, constantly covering new pools and having the stamina to keep going when others flag, increases the likelihood of a 'collision' with a 'vulnerable' fish.

The other is to study history and to seek out the experience of others. No one understands why a salmon rises to a fly, but knowing where and when a 'vulnerable' fish was caught before, and what fly fooled it, gives confidence it will happen again.

And because there is no ready answer to the puzzle of why a salmon takes a fly, there is a third option. Every fly fisher should experiment. Is an irresistible fly just waiting to be discovered?

A FRAGILE LIFECYCLE

All salmon lay their eggs in autumn or winter in nests or 'redds' that they dig in the gravel. These can be swept away by winter floods. Salmon fry emerge in the spring. This is the best time for the baby fish to find food as the natural world awakes, but most salmon streams are unproductive environments and competition for food is fierce. Only a tiny proportion find enough food, or escape their many predators, to mature a year or two later into 'smolts' that are ready to migrate to the sea. Here they face a physiological test as their body adapts to salt water. There are also new prey to find, new predators to avoid and a long migration to distant feeding grounds to face. No wonder the numbers of salmon that return to breed in their natal rivers each year are uncertain.

MAKING THEIR WAY UPSTREAM

There is a popular picture that adult salmon forge bravely upstream, against all odds, when they return to their home river. That is not quite the case. The best indicator of salmon runs is what happened last year, even if numbers cannot be guaranteed. Close to or north of the Arctic Circle, the available summer season when rivers are ice free is short, and salmon runs, including the timing of the arrival of the different species of Pacific Salmon, are fairly predictable. This is why you should plan carefully if you want to target a particular species, as their 'prime time' will be short.

Further south it is different. All the rivers in the British Isles have different salmon seasons even though only one species, the Atlantic Salmon, is involved. Some rivers have 'spring runs', others see no salmon until grilse run in the summer, while some have only autumn runs in September and October. A lucky few have all three runs.

Scientists believe each river system has its own unique gene pool which is reflected in the different runs of fish. This is the reason why, today, they are very reluctant to agree to the cross-river system stockings that were common until a few years ago.

Although last year's runs may be the best indicator of what will happen this year, the different timing of Atlantic Salmon runs is not permanent.

CYCLICAL CHANGES

Change tends to be slow, but annual catch data collected over many years show that spring runs and autumn runs tend to dominate in turn over a fifty-year cycle. Recent research in Russia, using data preserved by monasteries that depended on salmon catches in the rivers of the Kola Peninsula, also shows cyclical changes over centuries. There is speculation that earlier periods when catches were poor, even in northern Russia, were a reflection of periods of global warming. It seems current downturns in Atlantic Salmon numbers are nothing new and have the same cause.

RETURNING 'HOME'

Radio-tagging has revealed that salmon are programmed not just to return to their home river system but to actually return to breed in the very tiny stream or tributary where they themselves were born. This makes sense from an evolutionary point of view. With such a fragile and risky lifecycle, it makes sense to give your offspring the same start you had if you were one of the few to make it. The downside is that colonisation is slow of other tributaries in a river that may be equally suitable, but which for some reason are not populated.

Radio-tagging has also revealed that returning adult salmon can behave very differently. Some seem to find a wonderfully comfortable place to lie after they enter the river. They settle down there, perhaps for months, not even moving, when faced with floods or low water droughts, until they make a final move to their chosen breeding stream. Others never settle in one place and can migrate up and then downstream, even going back to sea. No one knows why.

DROUGHT AND LOW WATER

Observations and catch records show that, when faced with low water or a high river temperature, returning adult salmon often 'refuse' to run. Big numbers can build up in estuaries as they wait for a change in the weather. Some shoals may run a long way into river mouths with each tide but then return with it. This can mean river mouth nets enjoy a bonanza that leaves upstream sport fishers angry and frustrated. Other fish just seem to remain out at sea.

SALMON IN SALT WATER

The physiological changes that shut down the returning salmon's ability to digest food seem to kick in before they reach their river. There are plenty of places, such as Scotland's Western Isles, in which summer salmon numbers can build up where small shrunken rivers empty into shallow sea lochs and where fly fishers try to catch them. Some salmon are caught, but they are just as likely to treat every fly cast to them with disdain.

In fact, they are much more 'vulnerable' when the weather turns and they get into fresh water for the first time.

GETTING INTO BREEDING CONDITION

Delays to salmon runs do not stop the physical changes to adult salmon returning to breed.

Lilac-backed, silver-flanked salmon lose their newly minted look quickly. The Atlantic Salmons' colours become duller. Cock fish adopt a multi-coloured hue labelled as 'tartan' in Scotland. Their lower jaws develop an alarming hook or 'kype'.

The changes in Pacific Salmon are even more dramatic. Spawning Coho and Sockeye Salmon develop bright-red bodies, while Pinks are nicknamed 'Humpies' because males develop a prominent hump in front of their dorsal fin (see Figure 1).

These changes develop slowly in Atlantic Salmon that run in winter or early spring, and which can wait a year or more before they spawn, but they are rapid in fish that enter fresh water only shortly before eggs are laid.

Many fly fishers become snooty about catching salmon that are no longer 'fresh'. No one can deny that salmon that have been in fresh water for weeks are not as beautiful as those that have just arrived, but this argument is exaggerated. A mature salmon fights just as well as a fresh fish. No one objects to catching a big, in-season, September brown trout that has begun to take on its spawning livery, so why moan about a 'coloured' salmon?

Of course, no one wants to fish for a salmon over their spawning beds when their condition has deteriorated terribly. They should be left to make babies.

WHEN ARE SALMON 'VULNERABLE' TO A WELL-PRESENTED FLY?

Most salmon are impossible to catch on a fly most of the time! But at times in their journey upriver, the experience of generations of fly fishers tells you to be optimistic.

FRESH SALMON

One of the most vulnerable salmon is the fish that has entered the river proper for the first time and has begun its upstream journey. These bright-silver fish, still carrying tide-lice from their time in the salt, often run upstream quickly and can be caught many kilometres above the estuary, but whenever they stop, perhaps for only a minute or two, they often cannot resist a well-presented fly.

SALMON IN SHOALS

Salmon love each other's company and they often run in small shoals. Later these shoals will band together at times, so that considerable numbers assemble below obstructions like waterfalls or man-made dams or in 'holding' pools.

Fly fishers often see a pod of fresh salmon enter a pool when their presence is revealed by fish leaping or 'heading-and-tailing' as they escape the rapids below. A few minutes later, the same fish are leaping through the fast water in the neck of the pool. You will be unlucky not to be able to extract one of them as they pass you. 'Fresh' salmon running and resting together are particularly 'vulnerable'.

LOW TEMPERATURES

Salmon are a cold-water fish. In early season they enter rivers that can be much colder than the sea. This temperature shock slows their journey upstream. When it is particularly cold and the river water seems to be a mixture of suspended ice and melting snow, the salmon numbers will build up in the lowest reaches of a river, often below steep waterfalls and rapids. These are a 'temperature barrier'.

Salmon are unable to ascend these falls, including artificial 'salmon ladders' that may be built round them, when temperatures are low. The more formidable the falls, the higher the temperature has to be before salmon can ascend them. It may need to be as high as ten degrees centigrade. A big build-up in numbers is suddenly released as the 'magic' temperature is reached. The whole shoal runs upstream over a day or two.

Fortunately, the cold water does not inhibit the salmon's 'vulnerability' to a well-presented fly. At the lowest temperatures, around five degrees centigrade, the salmon can be moribund and lie deep in the pool, but they will take a fly if it can be fished down there too.

It is not surprising that some of the most famous, and productive, salmon pools in Scotland are below such temperature barriers. There is no better trigger of 'vulnerability' than cold water and plenty of fish!

THE CREAM OF THE SEASON

As the temperature increases, salmon become more active. When the water temperature reaches ten degrees centigrade, all barriers open up and salmon are much more inclined to 'rise' to a fly fished high in the water well above their heads.

In Scotland, this temperature is usually reached in late April or May and heralds the cream of the season. The fish are well spread through the river, they are still 'fresh', water levels are favourable and they are 'vulnerable' to flies fished with floating lines.

And, of course, there is no better time to enjoy glorious highland scenery and to see it awakening in the spring sunshine.

Later in the year, high summer will often bring drought and high water temperatures. The salmon are still there, but 'vulnerability' wanes. In autumn, the advancing year will see frosts, floods and longer, colder nights. The water temperature drops and the salmon, now displaying their breeding colours, become 'vulnerable' again.

Why do Alaska, Canada, Russia and Iceland provide the world's best salmon fishing? It is obvious. Fresh fish, large shoals and the 'perfect' conditions described are found throughout their short Arctic summer season.

FLOODS

Salmon fishers love floods. A flood after heavy rain encourages salmon to run. Fresh 'vulnerable' fish enter the river. As the example of Quillachan Pool on the River Findhorn described in Chapter 15 demonstrates, a flood also disrupts the resident salmon and pushes them into water where they too become 'vulnerable'. No doubt the rain has also lowered the water temperature, which is hugely welcome in summer. It is all good news!

The fly fisher may have to be patient. A big flood can lift the river over its banks so that it becomes a muddy torrent. Few salmon will be caught until the river begins to drop back and to clear.

Rivers have different characters. There is no rule about how clear they have to be before the salmon become 'vulnerable' again.

The only way to be sure you do not miss the moment they 'turn on' is to be fishing when it happens. This is important. Some 'spate' rivers fall quickly when the rain stops, and the period when salmon, especially residents, are 'vulnerable' can be very short.

On the River Findhorn, the trick is to fish short casts close to the bank in very coloured water using a big, bright-gold, yellow and red tube fly. Fish are caught even in the most unfavourable conditions, but the signal that the water is clearing and falling is when you see the first salmon rise back in the main stream. Prepare for action!

SUMMARY

The overriding message of this chapter is that the most important salmon fishing tactic is to be in the right place at the right time . . . and to fish in the right way!

◆ 'Fresh' salmon, newly arrived from the sea, are 'vulnerable'. Fish where you see them or can intercept them.

◆ Salmon are more 'vulnerable' when in shoals.

◆ Salmon in cold water are 'vulnerable', but you need to get the fly down to where they are lying.

◆ Floods bring in fresh salmon and disrupt residents. Target these 'vulnerable' fish. Fish before conditions are 'perfect' in order to be there when they are.

FOUR

WHERE TO FISH – AND FOR HOW MUCH

Few fly fishers are lucky enough to live on the banks of a salmon river they can fish when the fancy takes them or conditions are just right. For most, a week or few days salmon fishing is long planned. The joyful anticipation of these precious days, shared with friends, is an important part of the trip.

Fifty years ago, Scotland was the centre of the elite world of salmon fly fishing. Fly fishing was a technique practised mostly on the best 'beats' when the water was being warmed by summer sun.

Some of the world's wealthiest men also fly fished in Norway, and some of them were discovering Iceland too. Few Europeans travelled to Alaska where a few intrepid American fly fishers were opening up their Arctic state. Nobody travelled to Russia.

Today, large numbers of fly fishers cross the globe in pursuit of salmon. Many rivers are 'fly-only', and they are accessible. Exclusivity is still expensive.

This chapter does not tell you where to go. The choice varies from expensive rivers where success is almost guaranteed, to those where it is a rare event.

These are not necessarily 'good' or 'poor' venues. You need to choose a whole 'package' that suits your ambition, needs and pocket. The advice below helps.

WHO OWNS SALMON?

In Europe salmon fishing is the possession of riparian owners who, although subject to national or local laws, control who fishes for the salmon in 'their' river and how they do it. So anglers need a 'permit' or 'tenancy' from the owner, and they usually need a local authority or state fishing 'licence' too.

In the USA and Canada, pioneers and early settlers were often escaping the tyranny of a landed aristocracy, so it is unsurprising that rivers are open to all citizens who buy a licence to support the state body that conserves and regulates wild fish populations. Exclusivity here is either the result of local arrangements or isolation. You fly into many famous fishing lodges in Alaska.

FINDING SALMON FLY FISHING

Salmon fishing is a limited resource. Seasons are short. Demand for the best fishing is high.

The best way to select what you desire is to trust one of the sporting travel agents or outfitters that specialise in matching fishers to a lodge, location or accommodation that meets their needs (see Appendix One).

Of course, some believe the agent's 'cut' is excessive and take on the search, booking and travel arrangements themselves. This is the age of the Internet and this do-it-yourself approach is easier than it has ever been. It has opened up the ability of lodge owners and of anglers to sell and find last-minute bookings, bargains and extended seasons.

FISH PAL

For example, the excellent Fish Pal (www.fishpal.com) website provides an international portfolio of salmon fishing destinations. On this site you can compare prices, study catch records, see the whole range of salmon fishing opportunities, work out availability and find a last-minute vacancy. If you dig a little, you get a good idea of what may be a bargain and what is overpriced. This website and the opportunities it offers is a revolution for the salmon fishing consumer. But do not expect miracles. The website demonstrates that the best fishing is over-subscribed.

Choice is what the Fish Pal website provides. It is now much easier to find what is available. You can decide to put your name on a waiting list or you can find a sub-prime week on a historic Scottish river. This may be a better bet than a good week on a lesser one. Best of all, you may be able to find an occasional day, or two or three days, on a top beat at a prime time when prospects are good, due to a cancellation.

SCOTLAND

BACKGROUND

Forty years ago, most Scottish salmon fishing 'beats' were let by the week to a tenant who was allowed an agreed number of 'rods' and shared them with his family and friends. Most tenants coveted their fishing week as a happy constant in their life and their landlord offered them the same week each year, perhaps with some judicious shuffling to suit individual needs. Existing tenants got preference if they wanted an extra week or a change. Therefore there were few vacancies and those on any waiting list had to wait for 'dead men's shoes'. 'New' tenants were inevitably expected to take a less productive week at first and to seek 'promotion' in future years.

These arrangements still hold true on the best weeks on the top Scottish rivers, especially those where the owners retain many weeks' fishing, and are not focused on a financial return.

COMPETITION

Salmon fishing is a competitive business. Over recent years, due to falling catches, many regular tenants have abandoned Scotland in favour of Iceland and Alaska. Over recent decades, others have decamped to the rivers of Russia's Kola Peninsula, which have become accessible, and where the accommodation provided is less primitive than it was.

There have also been successful, and some less successful, timeshare ownership schemes in Scotland, which have closed beats to tenants.

The number of rods allowed to fish has crept up on many rented beats. The price has not dropped to reflect falling catches. Some regular clients are moving on.

CLUB AND ASSOCIATION WATERS

There is also salmon fishing in Scotland that is owned or rented by local fishing clubs and associations. Cheap 'day' tickets are usually available from them.

HOTEL WATER

Some hotels in Scotland also rent fishing for the exclusive use of their guests. This will not be as cheap as association water, but it provides guests with the opportunity to fish at short notice for a day or two.

Many association and hotel beats are just as productive as neighbouring 'private' water, but they may get busy, especially if conditions are favourable.

HOW MUCH DOES IT COST IN SCOTLAND ON PRIVATE BEATS?

The price is not the only factor that attracts a visiting angler to a country, river or particular beat. The scenery, the accommodation and the presence of friends will be just as important. But because salmon catch numbers are so well recorded everywhere, comparisons on a cost-per-salmon landed basis are usually possible. No one should book a salmon fishing trip without doing this calculation.

For example, the following is a non-scientific, random sample of some well-known private beats on the rivers Tay and Findhorn fished daily by a known number of rods. These beats are usually booked for at least three consecutive days.

Using their published, five-year average returns up to 2013, and selecting the three months when they had their best catches, it is possible to work out the average cost of the salmon caught.

RIVER TAY

On a lower Tay beat, a day's fishing in September, the best month, costs £430+VAT per rod. It is much cheaper to fish in other months, but the average cost per fish is pretty similar throughout the season at over £650 per salmon.

On a middle Tay beat, with lower catches throughout the year, the daily rent was less, but the average cost was still nearly £550 per fish. But this average figure is dragged down by the higher number of fish caught in September when the average cost drops to just under £400. In other words, the increase in cost of a day's fishing in September is less than might be expected, given the greater number of fish caught.

RIVER FINDHORN

Costs are different on the Findhorn. On two beats selected, prices change significantly through the season to reflect likely catches. This means the average cost per salmon over the best three summer months is pretty similar and there is not much difference between the two beats. On one, the calculated costs in each of the three months varied from £200–£260+VAT per fish, while on the other the range was £225–£280+VAT.

VALUE FOR MONEY

The Tay and the Findhorn are very different rivers. The former is the biggest river in Scotland and is almost always fishable. The Findhorn is an excellent 'spate' river, where the catch returns are consistently good over many years, but, depending on rainfall, every day is likely to be either feast or famine. You can experience three bad years on the trot while the party that takes the following week might enjoy bonanza on top of bonanza. A ten-year commitment averages it out!

You also have to remember that the Tay beats will have boats and full-time ghillies. On the Findhorn you will be given plenty of good advice about your beat, but you will have to pay more for a constant companion.

This is a snapshot, not a comprehensive survey, but if real estate agents can price a house on location and square footage, it is hardly surprising that fishery owners and their agents do the same.

The other purpose of these calculations is to provide you with a method of calculating the true price, if not the value, of the salmon fishing you are considering. Fisheries and lodges should be able to tell you the five-year rod average for any week you are considering or provide the data to let you work it out for yourself. It is only fair to consider a range of adjacent weeks and to look back over five years or so. Salmon runs and weather are notoriously unpredictable in some locations. Prime time dates are those with the most consistent returns.

HOW MUCH DOES IT COST ON ASSOCIATION WATER IN SCOTLAND?

On fishing club or association water it is impossible to calculate the cost per fish caught because records are not kept of how many members and day-ticket holders are fishing on any particular day. However, there are some remarkable similarities about the best 'open-to-all' clubs in Scotland.

The Forres Association (www.spanglefish.com/forresanglingasso ciation), which has a few kilometres of water on the Lower Findhorn, enjoys an average annual catch of over 300 salmon and grilse, mostly between April and August each year. Day tickets for visitors cost £30. The association has several hundred members, and while some catch quite a few fish, their website reports that nearly 200 of them record a blank year.

The Inverness Angling Club (www.invernessanglingclub.co.uk), which fishes the bottom beat of the River Ness, also records over 300 fish each season, which is close to an average of one each for its 350 or so members. The club also offers day tickets to visitors for £32.

The most famous, and most attractive, day-ticket salmon water in Scotland is run by a local club in Grantown-on-Spey (www.speyfish-ing-grantown.co.uk). Their annual catch is also around 300 salmon and grilse (there are also plenty of sea trout). A day ticket costs £50, but this is reduced to £30 if you fish for a week.

On all these waters, the local experts do well, usually because they spend a lot of time on the water! Given the right conditions, and fish, lots of members will be out. They will be very friendly and they will try hard to give their visitors a fair crack of the whip. You do not need to be a statistician to work out what your chances of success are. On average, and calculated by the number of day tickets you need to work through, a Scottish salmon from association or club water probably costs just as much as one from private, less heavily fished, beats upstream.

PRICE COMPARISONS

There is no doubt that the costs of Scottish fishing on a per salmon basis are high in comparison with some of its international rivals. This is compounded by the uncertain weather. During summer no tundra or glacial snowfields top up the Scottish rivers. Their levels can fall away to almost unfishable if there is no rain. Dry weather can continue into the autumn and can even ruin the fishing on the Tweed, Scotland's best and most expensive river.

Excessive rain, not unknown in Scotland, can cause dirty, raging floods which wipe out the chance of fly fishing success for days on end.

It is not surprising that some of the best-known international sporting travel agencies and outfitters are shunning Scottish salmon fishing. They encourage their wealthy clients to travel to Scotland for shooting instead, with fishing thrown in as a possible bonus.

AN EXAMPLE OF WHAT IS ON OFFER

Scotland does offer one unique salmon fishing experience: the traditional country house party. This option is available on many Scottish rivers.

RIVER LOCHY

For example, in Inverness-shire's River Lochy, fishing rights are owned by a long-standing syndicate of families, known as the River Lochy Association (www.riverlochy.co.uk). The fishing rights are not part of a great estate to be managed alongside the lands, tenancies and manifold other responsibilities. These people are in it because they love fishing. The ambience reflects this. A big effort is put into bankside maintenance, paths, huts and the creation of new lies in the river. But equal care is taken not to tame the wildness of the place. The fishery staff are as committed as the owners to making things even better.

The private beats on the Lochy take up all the 13-kilometre main stem of the river below the hydroelectric power station and fish ladder at Mucomir. This holds back the outflow from Loch Lochy and from the even larger Loch Arkaig beyond. Here, the river becomes the smaller River Spean, which, 16 kilometres upstream, is itself controlled by the Laggan Dam, which migratory fish cannot ascend. Halfway along the Spean, its major tributary, the Roy, breaks off. This long tributary is the major upstream breeding site for Lochy spring salmon and the main contributor to 'natural' rises and falls in the main river following rain. River Lochy Association bailiffs work hard to protect these spawning areas from unwelcome attention.

Four beats

There are only four private beats on the Lochy, and these rotate daily. This is the way it has been since the association was formed. Each four-rods party shares 3.5 kilometres of both banks of the river, and there are ten pools or more on each beat. You can take off in the morning to fish a few pools, confident that you will not see another human being until lunchtime when you meet your fellow rods, hopefully to share success.

On many other Scottish rivers, beats have been shortened, rod numbers increased, or you are always conscious of sharing a pool with someone on the opposite bank.

There are excellent ghillies on the Lochy, but they are not included in the rental. If you are new to the river you would be mad not to hire one and to share their secrets.

'Fly-only'

The other major plus is that the Lochy is a big, fly-only river. J. Ashley-Cooper described its standing as the 'queen of Scottish salmon rivers' alongside the Spey as Scotland's top fly fishers' rivers. Despite the ravages of hydroelectricity, it drains the whole west end of the Great Glen of Scotland and, at times, that is an awful lot of water. At normal summer height it tumbles rapidly past wide gravel banks but still needs a twenty-metre cast to cover some pools. It can only be crossed by boat. A big summer flood will lift it two metres above this level. Even at this height it will clear in less than twenty-four hours. Fishing time is never lost, even when you would be a brave man to attempt to take a boat across it.

The advantage of the dams that hold back water is that, after a wet spring, continuing electricity generation means a good level is maintained even when the summer is dry. Of course, as elsewhere in Scotland, a dry spring and summer results in low levels and difficult fishing, but, not surprisingly for a river overshadowed by Scotland's highest mountain, long droughts are rare. Twice as much rain falls on Fort William as falls on Aberdeen.

Fish run rapidly

There is, however, an inevitable downside to a big river with a short run to the sea. The Lochy is a salmon motorway. The fish run rapidly through the main river until the early autumn. You are dependent on a brief meeting with a travelling salmon or grilse. It is almost guaranteed to be fresh. The shoals of fish stock the river from the top. In 2007, the best recent year, the grilse were late but big runs arrived in late July. Catches were sporadic as shoals rested for only an hour or two in the downstream pools before racing for the tributaries. Some lucky souls were catching grilse after grilse from two pools full of leaping fish while friends on the adjacent beats bemoaned a lack of fish! It was mid-August before new shoals slowed down and took up residence in the lower pools and all beats were catching fish every day. The river manager believes that in September many salmon that have run through the main stem fall back into the Lochy pools where they will eventually spawn. There is a heavy demand for late-season tenancies!

Camisky Lodge
Salmon fishing tenants on the River Lochy can choose to stay in Camisky Lodge (www.camiskylodge.co.uk), a grand, slate-topped mansion, built one hundred years ago, which overlooks Beat Three.

A few years ago, the lodge underwent a complete 'makeover' and its former glory was restored. The house can accommodate a big family if you use all the seven double bedrooms (three en suite and one with a four-poster). You do not have to fill a house this size, but there are four sitting rooms, including one each dedicated to TV and the Internet, so you can all get out of each other's way. There is also a terrace the size of a football pitch.

You could call in staff to cater in such a house. It would be fitting in a house that boasts, across the corridor from the dining room, a butler's pantry. It is the size of the average urban kitchen and nearly as well equipped. There is an alternative, which is perhaps more fun. Over the week, appoint one or two members of the party to take on the full responsibility for preparing, serving and clearing away just one evening meal during the week. This includes providing the aperitifs, wine and any other dinner party goodies.

This can be a challenging evening for those on duty, especially if you invite guests. Eighteen people can sit comfortably round the candle-lit table in the magnificent dining room. And even the bravest cooks can feel slightly overwhelmed by a giant country kitchen and an unfamiliar four-oven AGA cooker! But the blessing is that this hard work is restricted to one evening. Everyone else is free to enjoy the deep sofas, the books and the huge sporting paintings that decorate the sitting rooms.

Of course, there is a danger that this approach to 'provisions' becomes a cooking competition, but you can draw up strict rules to prevent it. There are plenty of deep-freezers to aid advance preparation. Mind you, while the cooking has to be hearty rather than cordon bleu, it is wise to encourage sophisticated selections of wine!

The cost?

And what is the price of all this luxury? A peak week at Camisky Lodge costs, on a per head basis, well south of £150 each. Even if you add on the cost, just over £100 per day, for each of the four rods who rent a beat on the river, the total is still much less than the amount the average Brit spends on their annual holiday.

ENGLAND AND WALES

BACKGROUND

England and Wales are the poor relations as far as salmon fishing across the UK is concerned. In part this is because much salmon fishing is in private hands, or leased to fishing clubs that do not cater for visitors. Some hotels such as the excellent Arundel Arms at Lifton in Devon's Tamar valley (www.arundelarms.com) pride themselves on the salmon fishing they can provide, but, overall, England and Wales have never been an international salmon fishing 'destination' like Scotland.

This may be unfair.

ENGLAND

England's salmon fishing has undergone a small revolution in the latter half of the twentieth century. Some rivers in the south of England such as the Hampshire Avon and the Wye have seen salmon catches plummet, but some northern rivers have greatly improved. The Tyne and the Wear in north-east England, which were both heavily polluted for over a century, have been cleaned up and re-stocked with salmon.

The Tyne is continuing to improve and may soon achieve catches that equal its pre-industrial glory. This is a trend to watch. It is now the most prolific salmon fishery in England and Wales.

Much of the Tyne's salmon fishing takes place in the last two months of the season in September and October. A good proportion of the river is in private hands, but good salmon fly fishing is available for those prepared to search for it.

Use the Internet! Salmon fishing on the Tyne has not been commercialized, so you have got to search it out for yourself. A good place to start is the Riverdale Hall Hotel in Bellingham, Northumberland (www.riverdalehallhotel.co.uk). Salmon fly fishing is available there from £35 per day.

WALES
Many rivers in Wales (see www.fishing.visitwales.com) offer salmon fishing, usually by day tickets issued by clubs. The best rivers are the Towy, the Teifi and the Welsh Dee.

Licences
If you fish in England or Wales, you need an Environment Agency licence. Full details are found on their website (www.gov.uk/fishing-licences).

NORWAY

BACKGROUND
Norway, the home of giant salmon, boasts an amazing number of salmon streams. Some are huge, snow-fed rivers, but many are small, intimate and tree-lined. There are rivers with strong grilse runs as well

as those famous for much bigger fish. For information, visit www.visitnorway.com/fishing-in-norway.

There is a complex mix of private and public ownership of salmon fishing rights in Norway and bureaucratic arrangements for access, including lotteries for some beats, that even Norwegians struggle to understand.

So, if you want to go to Norway to fly fish for salmon, you are strongly advised to use the services of one of the many sporting agents who specialize in Norwegian holidays such as Frontiers (www.frontierstrvl.co.uk or www.frontierstravel.com). They will find you the size of river, fishing arrangements and accommodation that matches your aspirations and fitness! Some Norwegian fishing planned in the hope of connecting with a big fish can be hard work. Be warned!

AN EXAMPLE

The River Gaula, which flows into Trondheim fjord, is a long, multi-faceted river that flows from high mountain plateaus through canyons, forest and farmland. Its charms and its big salmon bring the same fly fishers back year after year. Twelve prime beats in the middle reaches of the river are managed by Gaula Fly Fishing Friends (GFF) (www.gaulaflyfishing.no).

These beats are above the famous Gaulfoss rapids on the river, which act as a temperature barrier to running salmon during the early weeks of the season. Plan to fish during the prime weeks from mid-June to mid-July if you can. By this time the spring snow melt is over, the river level has dropped and the water temperature is perfect for fly fishing.

Each beat has one or two long pools and is allocated to two rods subject to a six-hour rotation over a twenty-four hour period so that everyone gets a shot at all the pools. Some offer a better chance than others, depending on water height. The pools vary enormously in character. A competent fly fisher copes easily with the wading and casting necessary to cover them properly. An expert guide, Jonas Hammarstedt, looks after all the anglers who rent a week's fishing.

The Gaula is a big salmon river and most use fly tackle they are confident will ensure they can tackle a giant fish in a fast-flowing river. This means a fourteen or fifteen-foot double-handed rod and a range of shooting heads and sinking poly-leaders used with floating lines. Leaders are usually 6.8 to 11 kg breaking-strain fluorocarbon to handle big flies up to twelve-centimetre long. Good patterns are the Sunray Shadow or Black and Green cone head tube flies.

As the season progresses, the fishing can become more delicate and shorter rods and smaller flies come into play.

You can book accommodation at Bogen Farmhouse, which has been providing hospitality to pioneering English anglers since the 1830s.

The cost of a week, including accommodation, is around £1500. In addition, you need a Norwegian fishing licence (£25) and your tackle has to be disinfected (£15) as a precaution against parasitic contamination. Most visitors fly into Trondheim Airport. A hire car is also essential as the beats are spread over a 16-kilometre radius.

The Gaula is a big salmon river but there are not large numbers of fish. Even if you catch nothing, you give yourself a chance of the fish of a lifetime. That's a rare privilege.

RUSSIA

BACKGROUND

The salmon rivers of the Kola Peninsula in north-west Siberia are the most recent international salmon fishing destination. They have only been opened up, protected and managed for sport fishing since the fall of Communism in Russia. The prize of the best Atlantic Salmon fishing on the planet has inspired successful cooperation between local interests and Western investors. The website of the Ponoi River Company (www.ponoiriver.com) highlights the best example.

More and more Kola rivers are being opened up to anglers. Prices are high but stable. Bargains are sometimes available as seasons are extended to their limits. The season is short in the high Arctic. You are taking a chance with the weather and river conditions if you fish at the edge of the season, away from the prime weeks when success is guaranteed and prices peak.

No two rivers on the Kola are similar and their runs of fish are characteristic. The Ponoi has immense runs of grilse. A more northern river such as the Kharlovka is famous for bigger, but fewer, salmon. As ever, research carefully before you choose.

HOW DO I GET THERE?

Kola Peninsula is true wilderness. Access to fishing is only possible via sporting travel agents (see Appendix One) or owning companies. There is strong competition between the agents looking to persuade you to visit Russia, so you can be assured of good service and an efficient 'package'. You should investigate every element of this deal. The catch records for any chosen week will be clear, but you also have to ensure you understand the full picture. Ask about the weather expected, how far you will have to walk, the wading, the guiding arrangements and the accommodation. Almost everybody's wishes and level of competence can be catered for, but some rivers are much more suited to those who are fit and active. Do not spoil the trip of a lifetime by taking on more than you are able. Think hard about whether you want easy fly fishing and huge numbers of grilse or challenging fishing and a chance of a big fish.

AN EXAMPLE

One of Kola's most famous river systems, the Kharlovka, is operated through the Atlantic Salmon Reserve or ASR (www.kharlova.com). There are two main camps, the Rynda/Zolotaya and the Kharlova/Litza. From the middle of August, they are combined, but earlier in the year are run as two separate camps in order to access all the rivers in the system effectively.

Rynda is a medium-sized river, fast-flowing and divided by three waterfalls. By the end of June the whole system is usually well stocked with salmon. Fourteen- and fifteen-foot double-handed fly rods are used by everybody. The Zolotaya is a small river and ten- to twelve-foot rods are adequate.

Kharlovka and Litza are big rivers with big flows. The Litza falls are impassable to salmon, while falls on the Kharlovka usually hold fish up until late July. After that, many kilometres of additional fishing are opened up above the falls. Fifteen-foot double-handed fly rods, combined with shooting head lines, are the norm.

'Rock-hopping'

Wading is tricky everywhere! However, much of the river is accessible from the bank and 'rock-hopping', i.e. finding a convenient stance then lengthening the line to the maximum you can manage before moving down to the next rock, is common practice. The guides, who look after two anglers each day, have amazing wading skills. They take your safety seriously. The standard weekly tip is US $300 for the guide and the same for the helpful camp staff.

The landscape is typical barren tundra, but the Zolotaya is picturesque, with more foliage and flowers than the usual stunted birches.

ASR takes conservation seriously; all fish are returned and there are armed poaching patrols throughout the year. If you smoke you are not allowed to drop your butts on the bank or river. The river banks are pristine!

Helicopters

Access to and from allocated beats, decided by a draw on arrival, is by helicopter, although it is possible to stay out overnight in tented camps. There is no over-fishing of the pools. It is the land of the midnight sun and the 'home' pools near the camp can be fished into the night if you have the energy.

Everyone has their own cabin, with en-suite shower. Every comfort is provided for. There is a communal dining room, and excellent food with alcoholic beverages thrown in.

'Osenka' Salmon

These are big fish rivers. You would be disappointed if you did not catch a 9-kg specimen if you fished during the first six weeks of the season up to the end of June. Later in the season there is a grilse run so average weights decrease, but the fish become more active on the surface and 'hitched' flies produce spectacular action. The average catch per rod is ten to twenty fish per week. ASR close the camp for two weeks in August to 'rest' the river before the famous run of 'Osenka' salmon arrive.

Cost?

ASR prices vary considerably depending on the rivers you fish and the week you choose. The first week of the season at the end of May on the Rynda is about US $4000 per rod. A prime week at the end of June on the Kharlovka is nearly US $21,000! Most would be satisfied with the sport offered just outside the peak weeks at about US $5000. There are even youth discounts if you would like to introduce one of your children to top-class salmon fly fishing.

You have to arrange your own flights to Helsinki and a night's accommodation there. ASR organize a private charter from Helsinki to Murmansk (US $1000) where you have to face up to the unnerving challenge from Russian customs. This can be as bad as obtaining a Russian visa. Bags are easily 'lost', so divide your tackle among them. After Murmansk, everything else is fully inclusive.

On a per-fish-caught basis, Kharlovka salmon cost about US $250 each. Most ASR customers return each year so they clearly believe they get value for money. They think they have discovered the best fishing on the Kola and, by definition, the best Atlantic Salmon fly fishing in the world!

IRELAND

BACKGROUND

Ireland, along with Scotland, used to be a popular destination for English salmon fishers. It fell out of favour when salmon and sea trout catches fell sharply in the 1980s and 90s, in part due to salmon farming in open sea cages right along the Atlantic coast and significant high seas netting.

Unlike Scotland, and despite their economic woes, Ireland has turned a corner. Commercial salmon fishing has been reduced and in-river populations are now closely monitored. Many rivers are now totally catch-and-release, an anathema to many local anglers, in an effort to return their populations to healthy and sustainable levels. It seems to be working. This is a trend to be followed.

Where to try?

Ireland's charm as a salmon destination lies in the variety of fishing available. You can fish, with an audience, in the centre of Galway City and in Ballina on the River Moy in County Mayo. You can head for what was once a great country estate encompassing a whole river system, such as the welcoming historic hotel Delphi Lodge (www.delphilodge.ie) or Ballynahinch Castle (www.ballynahinch-castle.com). Or you can buy a day ticket at a modest price from a local fishing club.

The Irish tourist industry now understands the contribution fishing makes to the economy of the country. A valuable website (www.fishinginireland.info) should be your first port of call. It will direct you to many Irish salmon fisheries and has the great advantage of providing up-to-date information from around the country.

AN EXAMPLE

Irish rivers come in many sizes, and some of the biggest rivers such as the Cork Blackwater and the Moy attract many visitors. Ireland has been slow at restricting rivers to 'fly-only', in part because some of the big rivers have long, slow stretches where salmon gather that are usually unsuitable for fly fishing, and bait fishing can dominate. This is not true on the smaller spate rivers which can give exceptional sport, but only when conditions are right – at a modest price.

An excellent example is the Owenmore River at Bangor Erris in Co. Mayo. Several kilometres of this pretty, fly-only river are lovingly looked after by the Bangor Erris Angling Club (www.bangorerris angling.com).

Visit in September and pray for rain. The river is totally 'catch-and-release'. An Irish salmon licence will cost about €40, and a day ticket will be about €35.

ICELAND

BACKGROUND

Fish are the mainstay of Iceland's economy, especially since the collapse of their banking industry in 2008. Although many Icelanders have links to commercial fishing, they all realize that salmon-filled rivers are a valuable resource. Salmon are not harvested in the sea around Iceland.

Iceland is 'the land of ice and fire' and is one of the most active volcanic regions in the world. Much of it looks like a wild, unfinished wilderness, but do not be fooled; Iceland offers some of the most sophisticated and productive salmon fishing packages in the world.

Many Icelandic rivers are fairly small but most are fast flowing and add an exciting element to the dramatic scenery. Most are grilse dominated. Single-handed fly rods are often all that is required.

A few rivers have good runs of bigger salmon. The season is fairly short; often rivers do not get going until late June and their peak is past by late August.

In 2014, grilse catches around the north Atlantic were universally poor, including in Iceland. Hopefully this is just a one-off, but if it becomes a trend, Iceland would suffer because catches are grilse dominated.

FINDING FISHING

It is no good travelling to Iceland in the hope of finding easy access to salmon fishing. Even the official tourist board, 'Visit Iceland', websites are unhelpful.

In short, Icelandic salmon fishing is found through the international sporting travel agencies (and one or two Icelandic companies) that also manage most access to Russia, as detailed in Appendix One.

Competitive business

This is a competitive business, marketing an expensive product, so if you are planning a trip to Iceland you should compare the packages on offer very carefully to ensure the river you choose, from the many available, is of the size and ambience that suits you. Beats will always be long with many and varied pools to explore. Low water or high temperatures are rare. Careful records are kept, so you should be given a clear indication of likely results. You can be sure that the accommodation that will form part of the package will be luxurious. Riverside lodges are to the highest standard, with exceptional cuisine on offer. Guides are attentive and hard-working.

Rod-sharing

Local rules divide the fishing day into two sessions with a long midday break in which to enjoy the wonderful food and perhaps take a siesta. However, when fishing starts again, the guides are usually hard taskmasters and expect you to fish hard until 10 p.m., when the fishing day officially ends. It is a long day as they will also have got you up for a 6 a.m. start! It is, perhaps, not surprising that rod-sharing is popular in Iceland.

Non-fishing family and friends

Non-fishing friends and partners are also welcomed at most lodges, and the long midday break means you see more of each other than elsewhere and there is plenty of wildlife to see and scenery to explore. The usual fishing package is three days, and couples often combine fishing with a longer stay in Iceland to see whales or take part in the unique range of tourist activities on offer.

Reykjavik is a very lively capital city. And visiting Iceland has none of the hassle experienced in Russia. After arrival at a slick, modern airport, you will be quickly transported to your chosen lodge. Even if it is a long trip by road, it will be comfortable and there will be much to see. None of this comes cheap. This is another reason why rod-sharing, sometimes at no extra cost for two of you, is often favoured.

An example

The Fly Fisher Group (www.flyfishergroup.com) may be able get you a slot on the Midfjardara. It is the perfect Icelandic river. It offers small, intimate pools between waterfalls in one stretch or complex steams and shallows in the next. It is full of fish, mostly grilse, that are keen to attack small 'hitched' tubes in crystal-clear water.

The river is in northwest Iceland. It is a three-hour drive from the airport. The lodge has been refurbished and includes a Jacuzzi to help you relieve the strain playing fish after fish. Rod-sharing is welcomed.

Prime time is August. Expect to pay about £1000 per day for an all-inclusive package over three days. It is expensive, but just imagine what it would cost to enjoy exclusive and luxurious, boutique-style accommodation with cordon bleu cooking in one of the world's most unspoiled environments without the world's best salmon fishing. And, if you catch four salmon per day, it is cheaper than Scotland on a cost-per-fish basis.

ALASKA AND CANADA

BACKGROUND

It looks weird to lump together Alaska, an immense wilderness, and Canada, an immense country, but they do things differently across the pond.

Salmon fishing in North America is publicly owned, so as long as you buy an inexpensive licence, and obey local rules, you are free to fish where you please. Visiting anglers are welcome too.

Of course, you still have to get to the river. In Alaska, British Columbia and eastern Canada, there are thousands of kilometres of salmon rivers that you can access by road, by canoe or on foot, but there is a lot more that is so far from 'civilization' that to fish there you need to be flown out and accommodated in a lodge or camp that specializes in providing world-class fishing for wealthy salmon anglers from around the world.

The price of such luxury packages is not very different from other world-class fishing in Russia or Iceland.

Local knowledge

If you cannot afford to be flown into the wilderness, you have no choice but to buy your licence and search out a spot you can access where there are salmon to be caught. Anglers are like salmon; they shoal together, so it is not unusual to drive a long way along unmarked roads to find that the 'secret' pools you have targeted have also been 'discovered' by others. They may be standing shoulder to shoulder chucking spinners across the river and catching salmon, but the keen fly fisher needs a little more space. In truth, most of us want a little piece of wilderness to ourselves.

So, the most important skill is the ability to surf the many helpful official websites such as those from the Alaskan Department of Fish and Game (www.adfg.alaska.gov) or the Newfoundland Department of Fisheries and Ocean (www.nfl.dfo-mpo.gc.ca). As important are the many other fishing websites and blogs that make up 'local knowledge'.

In short, if you are a stranger you need a local, licensed guide. The best local guides often work through local networks of fishing tackle stores and hotels. The best gain a reputation that means they get booked up early. As ever, the more planning and research you do, the more likely you are to find the wilderness fishing you crave.

You do not have to be wealthy to find wonderful salmon fly fishing in Alaska, the north-western States of the USA, or western and eastern Canada, but you do need to work hard to find it.

Wilderness lodges

If you are wealthy, hundreds of sporting travel agents and lodge owners compete strongly to find you a lodge that you fly out to for a week that provides world-class fishing.

You need to be clear about what you want. What salmon species do you want to catch? Do you prefer a big river or a small stream? Do you want to fly out daily or drift downstream between tented camps?

An example

The Atlantic Salmon rivers of eastern Canada, such as the Restigouche and the Bonaventure, have stirred the imagination of salmon fly fishers for over a hundred years. Although originally opened up by English visitors, the majority of visitors to these rivers are now from the USA. They stay in some of the world's most attractive and historic fishing lodges. This part of the world is famous for rivers that are 'gin-clear' and where individual salmon can be seen, stalked and, sometimes, be persuaded to rise to a dead-drift dry fly.

NEWFOUNDLAND, EASTERN CANADA

The dry fly is regularly successful at Grey River Lodge in Newfoundland (www.flyfishinggreyriver.com). They get you there by helicopter. The accommodation and scenery are stunning. Two luxurious lodges take a maximum of only eight and four people who enjoy outstanding grilse fishing from mid-June to mid-July. Most fish carry sea-lice. The normal package is a five-night stay, which costs around $4000. This includes all ground and helicopter transport, meals and accommo- dation, fishing licence and taxes. In 2009, a good year, the fifty-five guests caught a total of 391 salmon, which is an average of just over seven per guest. Not surprisingly, Grey River Lodge has a large pro- portion of regular, repeat guests each year. If you can get in, this is a great deal!

ALASKA

It is almost impossible to pick out one Alaskan fishing lodge from the hundreds that are available and the range of salmon fishing they offer. It helps to divide the short Alaskan summer into the King, Mixed species, and Silver Salmon seasons. There are three types of lodges: full fly-out lodges, fixed camps located on a river and float-trip operations with camping. All have benefits, but some do not suit everybody.

For the real wilderness experience of North Alaska, you could head to Nakalilok Bay with Alaskan Wilderness Safaris (www.rod gunresources.com). This camp is close to the sea, and the plane from Anchorage has to land on the beach. From mid-August through September, it offers mind-blowing fishing for mint-fresh 2.7 to 3.2 kg Silver (Coho) salmon. You should catch thirty or forty in a week, alongside other species. The accommodation in tents is not luxurious, but aren't you there to get away from it all? There is gourmet cooking. This is a place for fishers who are young at heart, perhaps for a whole family. There is plenty of hiking and wildlife-watching for non-fishers. The maximum number of visitors is nine.

The cost is around $6000 per person for a week, all-inclusive. It is a bargain on a cost-per-fish basis.

SUMMARY

Salmon fly fishing is available around the world. When choosing, be ruthlessly honest with yourself about what you want. Careful research and planning are richly rewarded. Calculating the cost on a likely per-fish-caught basis is sometimes a useful measure.

◆ Cheap salmon fishing is available on association and club water in Scotland, Wales and Ireland. Or simply by buying a fishing licence in America and Canada. Advance planning is vital!

◆ Scotland offers the ultimate country-house experience.

◆ Norway is the big Atlantic Salmon destination. They are hard won.

◆ Kola Peninsula offers the world's best Atlantic Salmon fly fishing. Choose your river carefully.

◆ Iceland provides the most luxurious, easy-to-get-there, family-friendly, small river salmon fly fishing.

◆ Alaska has a huge range of Pacific Salmon fly fishing opportunities. And some amazing wilderness experiences are thrown in for free!

The more you 'invest' in salmon fly fishing, the cheaper it is on a per-fish-caught basis.

FIVE

GHILLIES, GUIDES AND COACHES

In his charming autobiography, Memoirs of a Ghillie, *Gregor MacKenzie tells of his first job as a teenage boy in the early years of the twentieth century. He was appointed to serve an Indian maharajah who rented the romantic Inverlochy Castle and the salmon fishings on the rivers Lochy and Spean in Inverness-shire for the season. His new master arrived in early March.*

Gregor's first task was to fish each day in the cold, rushing stream below the magnificent Mucomir Falls where the River Lochy roared down out of Loch Lochy, the southernmost loch of Scotland's Great Glen, while his master stayed warm and snug in the castle. The waterfall acted as a 'temperature barrier' that stopped spring salmon running further upstream. So when Gregor hooked his first fish he knew the spring run was under way and raced to tell his master it was time to start fishing.

The maharajah announced he would pay Gregor a gold sovereign for every salmon he caught that season. In those days, with abundant salmon stocks, this was a tidy sum for a country boy. Today, if Scottish ghillies were paid one pound sterling for every salmon caught from their beats, they would starve.

Then, as they mostly are today, Scottish and Irish ghillies were outdoor servants. They carried the rods, rowed the boats and maintained the huts and riverside paths. But, most of all, they study the salmon and their behaviour on their beat. They are not usually bold enough to tell you how to fish, but the more you ask them, the more they will help. The 'master's' role is to respect their wisdom.

GHILLIES

On the top salmon rivers of Scotland and Ireland, and especially on those beats where some fishing is done from boats, the rental package includes the welcome services of ghillies and/or boatmen. These men (they are nearly all men) are employees of the estate. Some will 'manage' the fishery on a full-time basis, but others will work on the river only during the season, perhaps reverting to other estate duties, such as game-keeping, in the winter.

In Gregor MacKenzie's early days every 'gentleman' would have a personal ghillie and there would be rivalry among the ghillies to serve the most successful 'rod'. Today some beats are now 'over-rodded', with more fishers than a few years ago. There is usually a beat ghillie charged with looking after all the rods the beat accommodates. This means an important part of the ghillie's role is to allocate the various pools and streams to the individual guests during each day and to try to ensure that, during their tenancy, all get fair access to the more productive spots. This can involve much tact and diplomacy.

DO YOU NEED A GHILLIE?

On lesser beats, ghillies may have become an optional extra. This makes sense for regular tenants who rent their favourite beat year after year. If they are fit enough to fish unaided, a ghillie cannot really help. They know as much about the secrets of the pools, where the resting salmon lie and how to winkle them out as any local ghillie. But if you are new to a particular beat and have never fished it before, you would be wise to pay extra to employ one. Even if you have a ghillie with you just for a day or two, it is your chance to plumb the depths of his knowledge and experience. Make sure the fishery/estate owner understands you want an expert fisherman to help you, not a manservant to carry your rod!

Most ghillies are competent fishers with a deep knowledge of their beat. The beat may not be extensive, so they should know every stone. They will see almost every fish caught so they know which lies are best at different water levels, which fly was successful yesterday and which combination of line and sinking poly-tip will present a fly at the 'right' depth.

Listen to their advice.

THE GHILLIE'S OTHER ROLE

The worst part of their job is being optimistic when they know conditions are pretty hopeless. Each new party turns up for their long-anticipated trip brimming with enthusiasm. They feel obliged to be cheerful but do not always succeed!

On even the most productive Scottish and Irish rivers, a drought and low water levels can be the kiss of death. Unfortunately, Great Britain's southerly latitude and Atlantic climate means there are no distant snowfields to keep levels up and to prevent the water becoming too hot in summer and autumn.

Perhaps this is why many ghillies display a wry sense of humour. Usually, they also maintain a store of local tales, not all about fishing, that are worth listening to. They befriend the children of regular tenants and they help them catch that wonderful, first-ever salmon. They can always recall the 'good' years when success came easily.

This happy, long-term relationship is the essence of Scottish salmon fishing. And ghillies value their role of maintaining tradition. For example, your ghillie may take you to a long pool and tell you to start fishing beside a large stone on which a white-breasted dipper regularly sits. He'll point out another stone hundreds of metres away at the tail of the pool and suggest you fish down all the way until you are level with it and your fly has reached the rough water below the tail of the pool.

Challenge tradition!

What the ghillie will not tell you is that it is only once in a blue moon that a salmon is hooked in the top half of the pool. Also, that nine out of ten of all the fish caught in the pool come from a short stretch in the lower half where boulders break the current and are a magnet for residents and for any running fish that pauses.

If you propose, as fish are scarce, that the best tactic may be to ignore the top half altogether and to fish the bottom half two or three times in your allotted time, concentrating hard on the most productive twenty yards or so to increase your chance of colliding with a vulnerable salmon, he will not demur. He may even compliment you on your expertise.

If you ask why he did not suggest these tactics in the first place, he will tell you that, for generations, the pool has been fished as a long walk between the two stones. And that is not for him to change.

GHILLIES ARE NOT CASTING COACHES

Similarly, you may admire the casting skills of your Scottish ghillie, but you should not expect them to be able to help a beginner. Very few of them have any training to enable them to coach beginners. There are many stories of youngsters, and others, given bad advice on the river bank that needed many hours of correction.

So, cherish the experience of fishing with traditional Scottish and Irish ghillies. It is a throwback to different days and may not last much longer. Remember it is a 'master and man' relationship and you may have to be assertive to get the best from it.

GUIDES

If you fish in Russia, Alaska, Canada or Iceland in a high-cost fishing lodge, you will be allocated to a guide.

These guys (men again!) are often professional fishing guides and may well have spent the northern winter helping anglers catch trout in the wilds of New Zealand or giant sea trout on the windswept island of Tierra del Fuego. Their role is, firstly, to protect you from the hazards of the wilderness but also to choose, perhaps from many kilometres of river(s), where you fish. They guide, you follow!

HIRING YOUR OWN GUIDE

If you employ a personal guide to help you on a wilderness trip, it should be done well in advance. Only book a guide that is 'licensed' by the state and follow up their references. After all, your success and safety will depend on his expertise.

In Newfoundland, in north-east Canada, it is illegal for a foreigner to go salmon fishing without a local guide. This may be a state project to enhance local employment prospects, but it may also save on emergency services call-outs. Dirt tracks through conifer forests and the rivers that wind through them all look the same as night falls, and it is easy to get hopelessly lost.

GETTING A 'GOOD' GUIDE

Alaska used to be seen as the land of the 'rip-off' merchants. But if you meet a stranger during a drinking session in an Anchorage bar who promises you the best salmon fishing in Alaska at a place only he knows, and you believe him, then you deserve to be ripped off.

LODGE GUIDES

Your relationship with the professional guides employed in the top lodges should be strong and enjoyable. Their employers want you to have a happy and successful trip so that you come back. Your success adds to their records of fish caught. These catches are what will persuade others to come for the first time. Your guide will be enthusiastic. This is why you may find them shaking you awake, despite your hangover, at five o'clock on a cold Icelandic morning. They expect you to be ready to start at six o'clock sharp, as the Icelandic 'rules' demand.

GET WHAT YOU WANT!

As professionals, guides quickly assess your fishing skills. They will choose pools and streams on the river that match your ability. But you do not have to be a passive follower. It is important for both of you to be clear about what you want. Do you want to catch as many salmon as possible or are you desperate for a big one? Do you want to try a particular technique, such as a 'riffling' or dry fly? Or do you want some time out to see and photograph wildlife?

Many anglers find bonding with their guide, and celebrating their 'shared' achievements, is the highlight of a fishing trip. Salmon fishing with a good, professional guide is a 'man and master' relationship. Embrace it.

COACHES

It is an unavoidable truth that you cannot begin to fly fish until you can cast. Learning to cast if you spin fish or are fishing with bait is easy and can be picked up in a few minutes. You may take longer to become an expert and accurate caster, but you will quickly be good enough to enjoy your day.

Fly casting is not as simple. Manipulating a long, tapered fly line through the air to deliver a weightless fly across a fast-flowing stream takes skill and practice. It is sad to watch beginners failing to cope. Their expensive day's salmon fishing is an exercise in frustration.

It is equally annoying for ghillies or guides. Their job is to ensure you do enjoy your day, not to teach you to cast, so they feel they are failing too.

Learn to cast before you get there! Use a fully qualified, licensed casting coach.

FLY CASTING LESSONS

The huge advantage of personal fly casting lessons with a coach is that they speed up the learning process. Once you understand what you are trying to achieve and your coach explains where you are going wrong, the rest is just practice.

The coach demonstrates the impact of the wind and river currents and teaches you how to cope. Coaches also give wise advice on rod and line choice and may save you lots of money. If you practise, as they advise, you will quickly develop 'muscle memory'. Like riding a bicycle, this new-found skill will never be forgotten.

Fly casting coaches are regularly approached by clients who plan to take up fly fishing in retirement who report they once learnt to cast in their teens but have not done it for fifty years. Imagine their delight when they pick up a rod and find they have not forgotten.

There is a downside to muscle memory. If you learn to cast badly, without professional help, you will struggle on difficult days or in awkward places. These bad habits can be hard to 'forget'. A good coach is essential to correct them.

PRACTISE!

Most fly fishing beginners have a short lesson with a coach and are then advised to practise what they have learnt for twenty minutes or so each day. Like learning to use a computer program, little and often embeds the new skill, much better than practising once a week. When it clicks, a return session with the coach gives a final polish.

JOIN A FLY FISHING COURSE

Another option is to join a beginner's salmon fishing course. These are organized by some fisheries, by individual coaches and by fishing magazines. Learning with others is always more fun than doing it alone. There is also a seamless transition from casting to learning to wade and to fish a fly. There is just a chance you might hook a salmon.

Sensibly, courses usually take place on rivers outside the prime season. After all, there is no point in spending a day or two practising casting and paying top dollar for fishing you hardly use.

FROM SINGLE-HANDED TO DOUBLE-HANDED RODS

Many competent fly casters with a single-handed fly rod assume they can pick up a double-handed salmon rod and will be able to use it in just the same way. The principles are the same, but adapting to using the long rod is not simple and many struggle badly. A short 'conversion' lesson with a coach makes for a painless transition. If you can, buy this lesson as part of purchasing and choosing your first double-handed rod. It may even save you money.

Some beginners question whether you can learn how to fly cast on a fast-flowing river, on the ponds or other places where many coaches give their lessons around the UK or in American cities. You can, and a good coach will be able to explain the impact of flowing water and the strong winds salmon fishers have to cope with.

To find a qualified angling coach in the UK, contact the Game Angling Instructors Association (GAIA). Their website is www.gameanglinginstructors.co.uk. There are equivalent state, or national, professional bodies in the USA, Canada and some European countries.

SUMMARY

- ◆ Full- or part-time ghillies and boatmen are employed on top Scottish salmon beats.
- ◆ Ghillies have huge knowledge of their beats but may hold strong traditional views about how to fish them.
- ◆ If a personal ghillie is an optional extra, consider hiring one for a day or two. Their experience could be invaluable.
- ◆ The guides employed by Alaskan and Canadian lodges and by Icelandic and Russian fisheries are seasoned professionals. Their role is to ensure your safety and maximize your catch. Take their advice!

◆ Few ghillies or guides are qualified fly casting coaches. Learn how to cast before you arrive.

◆ Fly casting lessons from a qualified coach are always a good investment. Being able to use a single-handed rod does not fully equip you to cast with a double-hander. Have a 'conversion' lesson.

SIX
THE TACKLE: RODS, REELS AND LINES

If you turn up at an Alaskan fishing lodge with a fifteen-foot double-handed salmon fly rod, most American guests will look on it with amazement. If you unpack a nine-foot single-handed fly rod on your first morning on a Scottish salmon beat, your ghillie will ask you politely, 'Where is your salmon rod, sir?' In the mid-Atlantic on Iceland's salmon rivers, and in Russia, these two cultures are mixing, and American rod-makers such as Sage and Loomis now make double-handed salmon fly rods.

The rivers on the Alaskan tundra often have wide banks and are surrounded by low scrub that does not impede a long back cast. Many Scottish rivers are tree-lined and overhead casting is often impossible. 'Spey casting', a form of roll casting which greatly reduces the space needed behind the caster, is the answer. 'Spey casting' demands a double-handed fly rod.

This chapter describes all the salmon fly rods, lines and other tackle in use today and leads you through the maze of choices.

RODS

Three types of fly rod are used for salmon around the world. Beginners should choose a rod commonly used where they are going to fish. It is easier to develop your new skills with help from companions that are familiar with the kit you are using.

In America and Canada this means a 'standard' nine-foot single-handed fly rod.

In Europe it will usually be a longer (thirteen- to fifteen-foot) double-handed rod.

A third type of fly rod has emerged recently. This is a Switch rod. These are light enough to cast with one hand although usually over ten feet in length. They have an extended handle so that you can 'switch' to a double-handed casting style at will.

Fly rods are universally labelled and measured in imperial units. Most other measurements in this book are metric.

Experienced salmon fly fishers usually buy more rods than they need. If they fish a wide range of rivers, they find a particular rod suits them best in different places. And they just like to own lots of fishing tackle! Even the most hard-nosed businessman seems to believe rod-makers' hype when the fishing bug bites. Be warned.

SINGLE-HANDED FLY RODS

The fly rod has to be matched to its job and to its owner. A long, heavy rod such as our forefathers used may be fine for a big strong man but would defeat a lesser being!

Why?

The critical element in every cast is a flexing rod tip that 'accelerates to a stop'. The 'stop' transfers this power into the unfurling line. Achieving optimum force depends on maximizing the tensile strength of the flexing rod. The single-handed fly rod is an extension of your forearm. It acts like a lever with your elbow as its fulcrum. As the rod 'accelerates to a stop', the wrist must be stiff. If it is not, it is like trying to cast with a broken rod.

ROD AND LINE RATING

Keeping a stiff wrist at this critical moment depends upon some forearm strength. Obviously, this develops with practice, but fly fishing is not a sport where bigger and stronger is inevitably better. Skill is required and this only develops if casting is not a constant test of strength. Beginners need a rod and fly line combination that is light enough to handle easily. The length of the rod is more important than its 'rating'. This makes sense. Lengthening the rod from, say, nine feet to ten feet makes a big difference to the forearm strength required to continually stiffen the wrist at the critical point in every cast during a long day's fishing.

Fly rods are internationally 'rated' and always labelled, say as '#7 weight'. This means the maker believes the rod should be matched with a #7 weight fly line labelled to the international American Fishing Tackle Manufacturers' (AFTM) standard.

Choosing a single-handed fly rod for salmon fishing is therefore a compromise. It has to be beefy enough to cast heavy line tips and large flies. It needs to be strong enough to play a big fish in a fast-flowing river. But it should not be so powerful that only a strong arm can use it all day.

The lightest fly rods rated up to #6 weight are used mostly by trout fishers.

You can get away with a #7 weight if your quarry are grilse or Pacific silver (Coho) salmon which are usually under 3.6 kg. If you expect bigger fish, a #8 weight makes more sense. If you are hoping for a big King (Chinook) or Atlantic multi sea-winter (MSW) salmon, a #9 weight rod should provide all the strength needed to defeat it. Remember, stick to a nine-footer unless you are a big man and happy to use a longer rod all day.

Trout fishers delight in using the lightest of rods and justify spending hundreds of pounds or dollars on expensive rods that are just a fraction lighter than their competitors. Heavier #8 weight (and above) rods are not such refined tools and there is a very limited advantage in the most expensive.

'ACTION'

It is not only length and weight that are important. If you're trying fly fishing for the first time, your rod should have an all-through middle-to-tip 'action', i.e. it should flex progressively from its tip to its middle so that you are able to 'feel' it bending as the acceleration of the rod tip and fly line build up the force of a cast. Later, you might advance to a stiffer, tip 'action' rod which will be more expensive and will provide more force for long casts but only in response to good technique.

Fortunately, the cheaper ranges of rods from reputable fishing tackle firms usually have a middle-to-tip action. This is the price range where a beginner should start. An excellent beginner's nine-inch #8 weight fly rod will cost around £75. Last year's model may be 'on offer' and even cheaper. Popular mid-range rods cost twice this amount.

DOUBLE-HANDED RODS

In the UK and Europe, nearly all salmon fly fishers use a double-handed rod and the commonest length purchased is fifteen feet. These are formidable tools and are usually rated for #10 or #11 weight fly lines. Using one of these rods is obviously greatly aided by the use of two hands, but even the lightest and most expensive demand lots of energy if used for a long day.

These rods are powerful and are able to lift the long 'heads' of specially designed fly lines into the air to execute 'Spey' casts. This is fine if you are fishing in the widest, lower reaches of Scotland's Tay or Tweed and need a 100-foot plus cast to cover the pools.

But if you are fishing in most of Scotland's rivers, which are more modest streams, you are seriously over-gunned if you use a fifteen-foot rod.

A thirteen-foot model, usually rated for #8 or #9 weight lines, is a much better option. If necessary, you will be able to 'Spey' cast a long way if you choose the correct line. You should also avoid the need to visit your chiropractor!

The advantage of a double-handed fly rod over a shorter single-handed rod is its ability to make long 'Spey' casts where no back cast is possible. To 'Spey' cast well, the long rod should flex down towards the butt when 'fully loaded'. This helps you to make a powerful 'roll cast' that curls the fly line high across the river. This 'middle-to-tip plus' rod action is difficult for rod builders to get right. Interestingly, in test after test conducted by fishing journals, it is not always the most expensive rods that are favoured by the expert casters involved.

It is wise to test several rods in your price range before buying. You should seek the services of an expert caster if you are a newcomer. Get the choice right and you will find a perfect partner that will probably last a lifetime. The amazing material technology breakthroughs of the last fifty years that have led us from heavy, slow-action built-cane through glass to modern, light carbon fibre rods are unlikely to occur again in the future.

SWITCH RODS

Switch rods were first designed for use on the Skagit River in western Canada. This is a narrow river where long casting is not required, but there are many sections where the bankside undergrowth prevents any back cast. These rods must be teamed up with special 'skagit' lines usually supplied as a package. The lines have a profile that aids 'Spey' casting and are weighted to match the chosen rod.

Switch rods would not normally be a beginner's first salmon fly rod, but learning to 'Spey' cast for the first time with these rod and lines is easy. They are certainly worth considering if your first salmon fishing adventure is on a smaller river anywhere in the world where long casting (i.e. more than twenty-five metres) is not necessary.

FLY LINES

To find your way through the maze of modern fly lines used by salmon fishers, it helps to understand the history of their development. Fifty years ago all fly lines were made of braided silk. The earliest lines were level, but it was soon realized that they unfurled more elegantly and gently if they tapered down to a fine tip. Tapered silk lines came in three sizes. They needed to be greased to float but did not sink far if they weren't. They rotted if they were left wet on a reel, so every fly fisher owned a four-pronged line dryer over which the expensive line was carefully wound in open turns after each day on the river.

Today, all fly lines consist of a smooth plastic coating over a braided-nylon core. You can buy floating lines, intermediate lines that sink very slowly, slow sinkers and a variety of fast sinkers.

Fly lines are cheap, but tough. Poor casting technique will damage them, but if they are regularly cleaned, they will last for years. It pays to buy best-quality fly lines.

The wide range of fly line sizes available is consistently rated across the world.

DOUBLE-TAPERED FLY LINES

The first plastic fly lines were expensive and most were 'double-tapered' (DT). Usually thirty metres long, a DT line has a taper at each end and a thick belly in between. DT lines can be reversed when the taper at one end becomes worn out. They are still used today by those who do not need to cast far, such as dry fly trout fishers, and others who like to save their money.

WEIGHT FORWARD FLY LINES

It was quickly realized that the large surface area of the thick belly of DT lines inhibited long casting, so the weight forward (WF) line evolved. 'Weight Forward' simply means that its first ten metres or head tapers towards its tip. The 'weight' of this head determines its rating. The rest of its full thirty metres is a much narrower shooting or running line that enables it to fly out easily. WF fly lines remain the standard fly lines used with single-handed fly rods today (see Figure 2). This is the line the new salmon fisher should buy to match their single-handed fly rod. On its box a WF #8 weight, floating fly line will have the shorthand label, 'WF8F'.

A floating WF fly line should be the salmon fisher's choice when fishing in the warm summer months. WF lines that sink are also

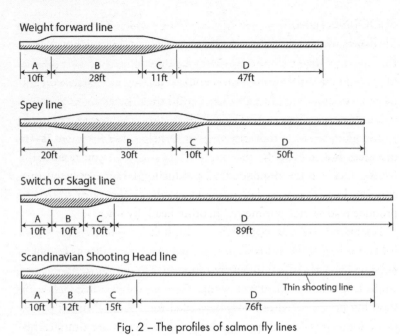

Fig. 2 – The profiles of salmon fly lines

available. They range from floating lines with a short sinking tip to whole length, very fast sinkers (up to seven inches per second in still water).

In running water even the fastest sinking lines will be held up by a rapid current and the salmon fly fisher who wants to get the fly close to the bottom has to experiment with different sinking lines and to ring the changes as the currents, depth and topography of a pool alter. Generally, it is easier to fish deep using sinking lines with a single-handed rod because the free hand is able to retrieve and manipulate the line. Sinking lines need to be almost fully retrieved and/or roll cast onto the surface after each cast. Trying to cast when the line is sunk is the surest way to break an expensive fly rod.

There will be much more on choosing, casting and fishing with sinking lines in Chapters 8–13.

SHOOTING HEADS

Fly fishers who were desperate to cast as far as possible quickly realized that the only way to do this was to make the shooting or running line of a weight forward line even thinner to reduce the surface tension as it passed through the rod rings. They cut off the first ten metres or so of a double-tapered line and attached this to a thin nylon monofilament running line. This innovation certainly helped achieve maximum distances but, inevitably, the running lines tangled constantly. The fishing tackle trade responded by producing a range of new, thin running lines that were less prone to tangling. They also started to produce ready-made ten-metre 'shooting head' fly lines.

For many years this approach was limited to trout fly fishers who fished from the banks of lakes and needed to get their flies as far out as possible. Recently, Scandinavian salmon fly anglers realized that they could fish flies deep in fast-flowing rivers by using a heavy sinking shooting head line with a double-handed rod. The technique was to make long casts, often upstream, to give the line more time to sink to the bottom before it tightened and started to swing round in the current. Again, fishing tackle companies were quick to catch on and many now sell 'Scandinavian-style' shooting head salmon fly lines and state-of-the-art running lines.

This is specialist kit. You should only think of following this fashion if you fish in the biggest, fastest-flowing salmon rivers in the colder months of the year when the fish are more moribund and unlikely to rise to a fly fished high in the water.

SPEY LINES

The ability to Spey cast using a double-handed rod can be essential on high-banked or tree-lined Scottish rivers. It is possible to Spey cast using either a double-tapered or WF line, but in recent years nearly all fishing tackle firms have introduced new 'Spey style' fly lines for this casting technique.

The Spey cast is an adapted roll cast and a WF line with a longer tip and the bulk of its weight further back along the head (see Figure 2) means an easier and more effective roll cast. Spey lines are made with different lengths of heads (see Figure 20). As Chapters 9 and 10 describe, these allow the caster to increase the amount of line in the air during the cast.

In practice, the salmon fly fishing beginner should choose a Spey fly line with a short head (approximately fifteen metres). The more accomplished caster will be able to handle a medium length head of nineteen metres but only the most expert can use the longest, which can be over 22 metres long. It is sad to see beginners struggling to use such lines. They have a place only on the widest rivers where there is plenty of space behind the caster or on the tournament casting field.

Spey lines are available as floating, sink-tip or 'intermediate' sinking lines. The beginner should stick to a floater. Spey casting is much more difficult using lines that sink, and you need to become competent using a floating line first.

Happily, Spey lines are just as easy to use for overhead casting with a double-handed salmon fly rod, so there is no need to buy any other type of WF line.

SKAGIT LINES

'Skagit' lines are a recent innovation designed to be used with Switch fly rods, either as single-handed rods for overhead casting, or double-handed for Spey casting.

Essentially, they are compressed Spey lines. The overall head length is only eight to nine metres, but they still have a long tip with the weight concentrated towards the rear of the head before the thick belly tapers steeply down into a long running line (see Figure 2). The result is a rod/line combination that can Spey cast as a double-hander in places where there is almost no space behind the caster, but a single-hander can also overhead cast a long way as if they are using a short shooting head line.

A Skagit line has its weight concentrated in a short length of line. It is vital that the line weight, or rating, is exactly matched to the Switch rod. They are usually sold as a package by manufacturers and this is the best way to ensure a perfect fit.

If you are going salmon fly fishing on a relatively small river where space may be limited, you will value a Switch rod and Skagit line.

LEADERS

Poly-coated leaders are made from 13.6 kg breaking-strain nylon monofilament line coated with polymers into which particles have been incorporated to increase their sinking rates. For salmon fly fishing, these 'leaders', which are usually four or five metres long come in four different sinking rates: intermediate, slow-sinking, fast-sinking and super-fast-sinking.

'Poly-leaders' attached to the end of fly lines are an essential part of the salmon fly fisher's armoury. They are often sold as part of a package with a floating fly line.

An important part of salmon fly fishing is presenting your fly at the 'right' depth, and, at the business end, fly fishing tackle often consists of a sinking poly-leader, transparent nylon or fluorocarbon leader and fly (see Figure 3).

An intermediate poly-leader attached to the tip of a floating fly line will not sink the leader very far, but it will be enough to stop the fly 'skating' across the surface in fast streams. Obviously, the other sinking poly-leaders will sink the leader and fly further.

Sometimes sinking poly-leaders are also attached to sinking fly lines. For example, a fast-sinking poly-leader attached to an intermediate or slow-sinking fly line will pull the fly down even deeper. In practice, there are many possible combinations (see Figure 3), but Chapter 12 explains that it is important not to over-complicate these options.

Tapered nylon monofilament leader and tippet

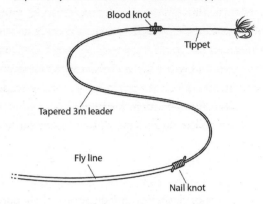

Fast sinking 4.5m poly-leader and tippet attached to braided loop on fly line

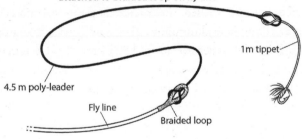

Slow sinking 1.5m poly-leader

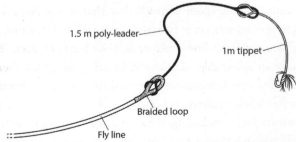

Fig. 3 – Different combinations of fly lines, sinking poly-leaders and fly

It is no good using the poly-leader to achieve the desired depth and having a long nylon or fluorocarbon leader which sinks much more slowly and will hold the fly up in the water. This part of the leader must be only a metre or so.

Floating, transparent poly-leaders are also available, but there is really no point in them. If you do not need a sinking leader, then attach a tapered, nylon monofilament leader plus 'tippet' to the end of your floating fly line. The next chapter gives advice on knots and other connections.

FLY REELS

Fishing reels are objects of desire. Spin fishers love their fixed spool and multiplying reels. These tactile, engineering gems, with their smooth gears and clutches, beg you to turn their handles. Fly fishers are offered designer-labelled, skeletal centre-pin reels engineered from a bar of aviation grade aluminium. They have a price to match.

Buy a beautiful expensive fly reel if you wish, but remember its main function is simply to store line. You will barely use it all day if you are a salmon fisher. Cheaper reels are just as effective at storing line.

CHECKS AND CLUTCHES

A salmon fly reel should have a 'wide-arbour' spool. It simply means that the centre of the spool is in-filled so that the backing line and fly line are not wound on it in tight turns which can cause similar 'memory' loops in the line when it is pulled off the reel. The reel should have an adjustable 'check' and 'clutch'. The spool then clicks as it turns. The clutch mechanism is used to control the tension and release of line when a salmon is being played.

All modern reels, including those of a modest price, share these features. If you inherited a reel from your grandfather, you may have to control the rotating spool with the flat of your hand. You may even find this is easier to do than to adjust the clutch on the costly modern equivalent.

LINE CAPACITY

The most important feature of a salmon fly reel is that it has the capacity to contain a thick, lengthy fly line and sufficient backing which you may need if you hook a big fish which makes a determined bid for freedom in fast water. About one hundred yards of backing line (usually Dacron or braided nylon) is enough. The thicker backing lines are easiest to handle but they do fill up the spool.

You need to buy spare spools (not additional complete reels!) for each fly line you buy. If you need several lines, the 'cassette' reels which come with a batch of spare, easily changed central spools are the best and cheapest option.

SALMON FLIES

There are thousands of different 'patterns' and sizes of salmon flies used across the world. All hooks, including salmon fly hooks, are sized on an international even number scale. The bigger the number, the smaller the hook. Sizes 0 to 6 are 'big' salmon flies. Size 8 flies tied on a hook 1.8cm long is probably the most commonly used size. In very low water, flies as small as size 14 are used occasionally. Hooks that are bigger than size 0 are 2/0, 4/0 etc. on the scale. Single hooks this big are still used to tie some traditional salmon flies (see Figure 4).

There is no 'magic' fly that works everywhere and which no salmon can resist.

Fishing would be boring if success was guaranteed, but the search for an ever better fly goes on. For generations salmon fly fishers have fished down pools that were 'full of fish' and caught nothing.

'Why won't they take my fly?' they ask as they scramble in their fly box to find a different one to offer. They are asking the wrong question.

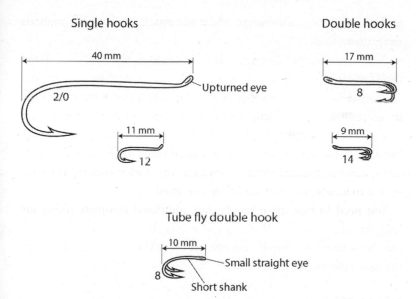

Fig. 4 – Salmon hooks – size comparisons

When salmon enter fresh water, their digestive system ceases to operate. They are physically unable to digest anything. Their stomachs are always empty. This is an impressive example of evolution by natural selection. If adult salmon, a large predatory fish, were hungry when they entered a river system, the food available would be juvenile salmon, their next generation. The survival of the species is probably dependent on this adaptation.

The correct question is, 'If salmon don't eat, why does one ever take a fly?'

This question goes to the heart of salmon fishing.

All other fishing is based on fooling a hungry fish. Go trout fishing and you know your quarry has to eat to live. You can observe what they eat if they are 'rising' to take floating flies. You can investigate the stomach contents of a fish you catch. You can tie an artificial fly that imitates what they are eating and fool the trout into believing your fly is the 'real thing'.

There is no equivalent tactic in salmon fly fishing. The tactics employed when choosing a fly are based on anglers' experience over hundreds of years, not upon a search for a more realistic imitation of a salmon's prey.

Perhaps a salmon rises to a fly out of aggression or because it is reminded of a prey animal it used to enjoy eating. No one knows.

Understanding the development of salmon flies over the last century helps to explain where we have got to today.

TRADITIONAL FLIES

In the nineteenth century, George M. Kelson created one of angling's most beautiful illustrated books, *The Salmon Fly. How to Dress It and How to Use It*. The pages detailed the wonderful patterns of 'fancy' salmon flies, large and small, which he insisted the Victorian salmon fly fisher needed. His biological knowledge was poor and he even wondered whether salmon rose to take drowned butterflies. Perhaps this is why the flies he described are so exotic. Brightly coloured, they use strips of feathers from rare birds like Amazonian macaws and toucans.

These 'traditional salmon flies' such as the Durham Ranger and Silver Doctor were often large flies tied on single hooks up to size 2/0 with upturned or gut eyes (see Figure 4). These 'heavy irons' were used on cold spring and autumn days because weighty flies sank well down in cold water behind slow-sinking silk lines. They were notoriously bad hookers and lots of salmon were hooked then lost when being played.

WADDINGTONS

Early in the twentieth century, Richard Waddington, another experienced fly fisher, also insisted that, in early spring and into autumn when temperatures dropped and river levels were high, salmon preferred a big fly fished deep. He introduced them to flies tied onto an inch or two of heavy wire to which a treble hook, which improved hooking effectiveness, was attached. He replaced the fine feathers of traditional flies with tough, dyed buck tail which he had seen used successfully in salmon flies used in Canada. These 'hair wing' flies became all the rage, especially for spring and autumn fishing, and rapidly led to the development of 'tube flies'. The buck tail was easy to dress onto a one- to two-inch tube (plastic, aluminium or brass to provide weight options) through which the leader was threaded before being attached to a separate hook. The tube/hook junction was covered with a short length of plastic or silicon tubing to keep fly and hook together (see Figure 26).

TUBE FLIES

Tube flies are still popular today but are mostly dressed on specially designed 'tubes' which are lined to protect the leader and into which a short-shanked hook fits snuggly. Modern fly fishers are less concerned about fly patterns than their predecessors, so do not demand a huge variety. Common combinations of buck tail 'wings' are black and yellow or red and yellow. The popular Willie Gunn pattern blends yellow, orange and black buck tail over a gold-ribbed black body.

When Richard Waddington was experimenting with new types of flies, there were few fly lines available. It was a real problem to get flies down deep enough in early spring and autumn. Therefore Waddingtons were tied on heavy wire mounts. Heavy brass tube flies also became popular.

Today, fast-sinking lines and shooting heads are used to get flies down deep, and heavy Waddingtons and brass tubes are redundant. You can achieve the same depth using fast-sinking fly lines and poly-leaders, a short nylon leader and a lighter fly. And casting lighter flies is much easier and less dangerous!

Most modern tube flies are tied onto plastic tubes (see Figure 26). A little weight can be added, if desired, by adding a small brass or tungsten 'cone' head.

The best place for big traditional size 1/0 'singles' is in a picture frame on the study wall rather than on the end of your leader.

SMALL BLACK FLIES

In the 1930s, a famously successful salmon fisher, A.H.E. Wood, who fished the Cairnton beat on Scotland's River Dee, convinced a generation of fly fishers that 'fancy' flies were unnecessary and that all you needed was a small black fly. He convinced himself that the more minimal the dressing, the better it was.

Cynics point out that the plentiful, tide-fresh salmon that populated Cairnton each May in those years would have been so eager to take a fly that almost anything on a hook would have caught them. But no one denies that a small black fly is still probably the most successful salmon fly used in Scotland today during the summer and early autumn.

MODERN SALMON FLY HOOKS

In the 1980s, all UK salmon caught by anglers were killed. Fly fishers hated a fish shedding the hook and escaping after being played for a time.

Esmund Drury, who invented the General Practitioner, an effective shrimp-style fly pattern, capitalized on these fears. He sold a black japanned treble fly hook with a traditional up-eye. Soon, nearly every salmon fly sold in Europe was on one of these E.D. Treble Hooks. It did not seem to matter to fly fishers, or the salmon, that these flies often seemed to be more hook than fly. They were a pain to dress if you tied your own flies. They never caught on in the USA or Canada.

Since then, declining catches, and responsible environmental stewardship led by anglers, created a continuing, and still increasing, culture of 'catch-and-release'. Flies tied on treble hooks are not easy to remove from a salmon's jaws and they have fallen out of favour. Today, most rod-caught salmon in the UK, and around the world, are returned unharmed.

Today, most salmon flies are tied on single or double hooks. 'Doubles' are favoured as the two hook points help the fly to swim on an even keel. Tube flies use specially designed short shank doubles (see Figure 4). They have small, neat eyes that fit inside the tube.

The salmon fly hooks of yesteryear made of a heavy japanned wire are still sold, primarily so that keen fly tiers can re-create the traditional Victorian patterns. They are strong but they can be difficult to keep sharp.

A new generation of modern, stronger, chemically sharpened hooks is now available. Use them! Poor hook penetration is the usual reason a hooked salmon comes adrift. Even if you planned to return it, losing a fish after days of effort is hard to bear.

OTHER KIT

A joy of salmon fly fishing is that you do not need lots of gear. You can set off for a morning's fishing armed with a rod, reel and line with a fly on the end. A small box of spare flies fits in your pocket, as does a spare reel spool if you think you might need to try an alternative fly line.

Why then is it such a challenge to stop buying too much gear?

As in many sports, there are always 'must-have' items on the market to tempt you. Every fly fisher on the planet cannot resist buying a few more flies when they visit their favourite fishing tackle store or website.

To get started, a rod, reel line and flies are the essential items. There are other wonderfully useful products and 'gizmos' that most fly fishers carry. A choice selection of them is listed in the next chapter.

A FLY FISHER'S WAISTCOAT

Everything you need can be carried in your pockets if you buy a 'fly fisher's waistcoat'. Today almost every fly fisher has one of these great inventions. A good one costs in the region of £50. An even better one that incorporates an automatic, self-inflating life-jacket costs more, but no money will be better spent. It might save your life. Salmon fly fishing is a game that is played in fast-flowing, cold northern rivers and anglers die doing it every year. Some lose their footing in a fast stream. Others have a heart attack, collapse and drown. Reduce the risk!

FISHING BAGS AND CLOTHING

You may need a fishing bag too, even if it is only to carry some food and drink. Do think about this. Wandering about with all your gear in your pockets, unencumbered by a heavy bag, is one of the joys of fly fishing.

Out of respect for a wild quarry that will be alarmed if it sees you, good anglers wear outdoor clothing in sensible muted colours. There is an industry that is dedicated to providing you with such apparel. It is all designed to keep you warm and dry. Do not forget that as you will be wearing chest-high waders, you will only need a short 'wading' jacket, not a long one which will trail in the water.

WADERS AND BOOTS

All salmon fly fishers have to wade. In small streams you may rarely get above your knees, but currents can be deceptively fast. In big rivers you are constantly tempted to take one step further and the water is constantly lapping the top of chest-high waders.

After your rod and line, the right waders are the most important kit you buy. Most fly fishers buy chest-high waders even if they fish small rivers as even they have deep sections and, like good boy scouts, they want to 'be prepared'.

Chapter 13 gives advice on the wide choice available.

A WADING STAFF

When you wade in a fast-flowing river where the current is strong and/ or the river bed feels like greased cannon balls, you need a wading staff. Tripods are stable! Wading is much easier if you can anchor a staff on the bottom before you move your two feet to climb or get round an obstacle.

Most fishing tackle firms sell wading staffs, but they are often not much use. What you need is a staff with plenty of weight or else you are constantly struggling to get it down to the river bed in fast-flowing water.

The best are simply a straight, strong stick about 140 cm long (it depends on your height) with a kilo or so of lead sheeting wrapped round the bottom end. A rubber cap of the sort supplied for walking sticks stops it clanging against the river bed and ending all chance of a stealthy approach to a pool. A hole drilled through the stick about 25 cm from the top end accommodates a strong cord secured by a knot and tied in a loop that fits over your head and across your chest (see Figure 5). This arrangement keeps the staff 'to hand' whenever you need it.

Such a staff is weighty and awkward airline luggage, so you may have to compromise and use a shop-bought version, some of which collapse for packing, if you are travelling to fish.

LANDING NET

The best way to land any lively fish is to use a landing net. Salmon fly fishing is a mobile game, so you need one that you can strap across your back. There are plenty on the market. Make sure it is big enough.

A word of warning: if you are fishing with a long double-handed fly rod, it is almost impossible, if you are fishing alone, to get a salmon into a net with a short handle like one you strap to your back. The long rod prevents you getting the fish close enough to you.

Cord

Waders

Lead sheeting
wrapped round
for weight

Rubber
ferrule

Fig. 5 – Using a wading stick

Therefore, ghillies and guides carry landing nets and help if they are with you.

If you are unaided, you will find it easier to 'beach' your fish. This is not the preferred way to land a salmon that is to be returned unharmed, so great care is needed. Chapter 19 tells you how to do it.

HEALTH AND SAFETY

There is a long list of hazards associated with fly fishing and enjoying the outdoor life. Fortunately, the actual risks are low and are avoided by common sense.

The biggest danger comes from slips, trips and falls, both in the water and out of it. Wear the correct footwear, use a stick and buy a fishing waistcoat that doubles as a life-jacket. Always carry a mobile phone if there is a signal available.

If you do fall into a deep river, even if you are not wearing a life-jacket, you are likely to survive if you act sensibly. Do not panic. Waterproof clothing and waders are full of air and act as buoyancy aids. Spread-eagle your arms and legs and lie on your back. This may sound wrong if you are just above a twenty-metre waterfall, but in most places just allowing yourself to drift downstream will soon deliver you to the river bank or shallower water. The worst thing to do is to turn over onto your face and attempt to swim.

There is a small risk of eye damage from casting, so always wear Polaroid sunglasses which, in any case, are an essential aid to see into clear water. In many salmon fishing locations, biting insects can be a severe nuisance. The best method of prevention is covering all exposed skin before they start biting you. Nets to cover the head and face are used where their numbers are worst. Antihistamine pills help to reduce inflammation.

More ominous is the risk from blood-sucking ticks which can attach to your skin and may not be obvious without close examination. If you find one, it needs to be removed using pliers to twist it round carefully to loosen its grip and ensure its head comes out too. In Scotland, many ticks are infected with Lyme's Disease which is most unpleasant and can even be fatal. If you find a tick on you, seek medical advice.

Probably the greatest health risk (both long and short term) is from the sun, even in the Arctic. Wear sensible clothing and use sunblock.

SUMMARY

◆ Choose a rod that matches the size of the river you fish.

◆ Double-handed fly rods are out of place on small rivers.

◆ Not all double-handed fly rods are good Spey casters.

◆ Switch rods are great for smaller streams and restricted spaces.

◆ Buy best-quality fly lines.

◆ Spey lines are the best match for double-handed rods.

◆ Shooting head lines are the best for distance.

◆ Modern sinking poly-leaders have become essential kit.

◆ Use a fishing waistcoat that incorporates an auto-inflatable life-jacket.

◆ A good wading staff is essential.

SEVEN

THE TACKLE: PUTTING IT ALL TOGETHER

Unless you are a beginner who is lucky enough to be salmon fly fishing in prime time in Russia, Iceland or Alaska, you will probably have to put in a lot of effort before you hook a salmon.

There is a difference between a field sport involving a wild quarry and a ball game like golf. When you play golf and your performance is less than perfect, it is hardly a total failure. You can still enjoy your game. When fly fishing, if your cast splashes down an elusive salmon may be scared away. If you cannot cast far enough, the salmon may not see your fly. You may choose the 'wrong' fly. You may fish the 'right' fly at the wrong speed or at the wrong depth so that it is ignored. Only one hundred per cent will do. Anything else is failure!

Even if you succeed and hook a fish, it still has to be landed. Every fisher has a tale of 'the one that got away'. Sometimes the cause is a blunt hook, but often it is a broken leader or failed knot.

Of course, in both golf and fly fishing there is always a new hole to play or a new cast to make. But, at the end of a round of golf, you have at least played the game. If you cannot catch a salmon, especially when others do, or one gets away, it hurts!

This chapter is aimed at beginners but it may help others. It describes all the knots a fly fisher must be able to tie. It also gives some hints, and suggests some items to carry, that help bridge the narrow gap between failure and success.

ASSEMBLING A SALMON FLY ROD

Not long ago, most fly rods were two-piece rods. Only the longest, such as salmon rods, were three-piece to make them manageable and to fit them into cars.

Today, most fly rods come in four pieces. A nine-foot rod can be fitted into a rod tube which is less than 75 cm, and which will go in a suitcase. A fifteen-foot double-handed salmon rod fits into a 1.25-metre tube. It certainly makes travelling a lot easier. It also means there is now a right way to assemble your new fly rod.

Before you put up your new fly rod for the first time, lightly wax the male ferrules using a small piece of a candle. This will prevent the ferrules sticking. Nothing is more frustrating, when you are tired after a day's fishing, than finding you cannot take your rod apart.

Put the small piece of candle in a little plastic bag and put it in the pocket of your new waistcoat. It will probably last a lifetime.

DO NOT SWISH IT AROUND!

Four-piece rods should be assembled by joining the tip and second sections first, then the final section(s) so that you end up with the butt section in your hand. The reason for this is obvious; if you do it in the reverse order you end up with the fragile tip in your hand and the heavy butt and rod handle swinging about in the wind. But beware. You still have to watch where the rod tip is. More rods are broken when they are being put together than when fishing. Do not swish it around. Not only can you bash it into something, you are putting an excessive strain on it when it is not throwing a line.

As you assemble the rod, make sure the rod rings, through which the line will be threaded, are in line.

TAPE THE JOINTS

Finally, it is vital to 'tape' the joints if you are using a double-handed rod. Salmon rods are usually left assembled for the duration of a trip and the joints of rods used for Spey casting have a tendency to loosen over a day or two. This is, by far, the commonest cause of rods fracturing during use, because the female ferrule rocks as it loosens. Most anglers use insulating tape out of their tool boxes, but you can buy

Scotch 3M Super 33+ Tape which stretches to shape and is specially recommended for rod joints.

THE REEL

Fly reels are designed to be either left- or right-hand wind. If you are right-handed, you will feel more comfortable when playing a large fish if you hold the rod in your right hand and wind the reel with your left hand. Fly reels are designed to wind in the line when the spool is turned anticlockwise. When wound in this direction, the ratchet on the reel is light and it clicks gently. When the reel spool is turned in a clockwise direction as line is removed when, for example, a hooked fish races away, a heavier ratchet or an adjustable clutch engages to help the fisher play the fish. Because most anglers are right-handed, the 'factory setting' for fly reels is left-hand wind.

If you are left-handed, the setting needs to be reversed. All new fly reels come with instructions on how to convert them from left-hand wind to right-hand wind before use. It is usually a simple process involving turning over and replacing part of the ratchet/clutch mechanism. If it is necessary, change it before you start to put the line on the reel.

LOADING BACKING ONTO THE REEL

A backing line has to be put on a reel before the fly line. Backing line is cheap, braided nylon which is supplied on spools of varying capacity. You need to put at least one hundred metres on your reel. Backing line is a reserve if you have to play a salmon that is powerful enough to run over thirty metres when hooked so that it pulls all the fly line from the reel. Plenty of salmon will 'run onto the backing' but few will run more than fifty metres. Everyone lives in hope!

The backing line serves another purpose. It builds up the diameter of the reel's spool before the fly line is wound on. A wide diameter spool reduces the 'memory' coils in the fly line that inevitably occur when the line is pulled off the spool after it has been stored there for some time. Modern fly lines are all designed to have the lowest possible memory, but it is impossible to remove it altogether. This is why all modern fly reels are designed with 'wide-arbour' spools.

Matching the size of reel and the fly line correctly means it should be easy to 'fill' the spool with the backing and the fly line. The reel maker usually specifies its capacity but the thickness of fly lines from different manufacturers does vary, therefore a little trial and error may be required. If you find you need to build the reel diameter up a little by using more than one hundred metres of backing, that is fine.

DO NOT OVERFILL THE REEL SPOOL

It is just as important to make sure the spool is not overfilled. What looks neatly filled, when the line is wound on carefully for the first time, can jam up when the spool unevenly fills. This is the last thing you want when you are playing a lively salmon.

To wind backing line onto the reel, it is easier if you first remove the spool of the fly reel from its cage to make it easier to tie the line to it. Thread the end of the backing line through the cage before tying it onto the spool. Some fly reels have a specially designed 'line guard' incorporated in the reel cage, but if you are not sure where to thread it, lay the cage on its back with the 'reel seat' (the 'foot' that enables it to be attached to the rod) uppermost and thread the line through the lower quadrant of the cage, from the left if left-hand wind or from the right if right-hand wind. This may seem elementary, but beginners are often seen struggling with the wrong set-up. The end of the backing line should then be attached to the spool using a 'Fisherman's Knot' (see Figure 6). This simple knot secures the backing tightly on to the spool. You then put the spool back into the reel cage.

TYING KNOTS

Although the Fisherman's Knot is an easy knot to tie, it is as frustratingly difficult as any other knot when you try for the first time.

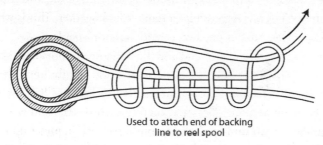

Used to attach end of backing
line to reel spool

Fig. 6 – Fisherman's knot – attaching backing line to the reel spool

Persevere! Soon you will be able to tie all the regular knots you use time after time with your eyes closed! Until you can do this, you will find knot-tying is easier if you hold the line against a dark background so that you can see what you are doing. It is also vitally important to coat each knot with your spit to lubricate it before it is tightened. Where two strands of line are joined, or the knot is forming a loop, spit on them first. The surface tension keeps the two strands together.

HELP FROM A FRIEND

To put the backing or a fly line onto the reel it helps to have a friend. They thread the backing line spool on a pencil and then hold it firmly, providing the correct tension, while you wind the length you need onto the reel.

If you are on your own, you will have to hold the pencil between your knees! Having a friend certainly makes the task easier. Your aim is to make sure the layer of backing line is evenly layered on the reel spool and is kept tight enough to create a firm base for the fly line to follow.

LOADING THE FLY LINE

The next step is to put the fly line on the reel. This has to be done carefully! A new fly line is packed in the factory in wide coils onto a two-piece plastic spool. It will be secured by small ties that need to be cut off. The correct end (i.e. the end of the 'running line') must be attached to the backing to ensure the line is correctly loaded on the reel. It is so easy to get this wrong that this end is usually labelled. Do not remove this helpful label until the end of the line is tied to the backing. Do not forget this end of the fly line also has to go through the correct opening or line guard in the reel cage.

There are two possible methods of joining the backing line to the fly line.

Nail knot

The first is by using a 'nail knot' (see Figure 7). Because fly line is slippery, the knot is made more secure by tying a single overhand knot in the end of the fly line and tightening the nail knot snugly against it. The nail knot is most easily tied using a large darning needle rather than a nail! The free end of the backing can be passed through the eye of the needle to be pulled through the loops.

The knot between the backing line and fly line is one you may hardly ever see again. But if the time you do see it is when the fly line is disappearing through the rod rings because you have hooked a giant salmon, the last thing you want is for it to jam there. Therefore, after the nail knot has been trimmed, coat it with some 'Zap-a-Gap' super-glue which will give it a smooth, slightly flexible surface. This brand of superglue, which has been specially designed for anglers, is available from any fishing tackle shop or website. You must wait for the glue to dry before finally loading the fly line.

Braided loops

The other joining option is to fit a 'braided nylon loop' onto the end of the fly line and to tie the backing line to this using a 'tucked half-blood' knot (see Figure 8). There are other knots, but the tucked half-blood is secure and is easier to tie than many others.

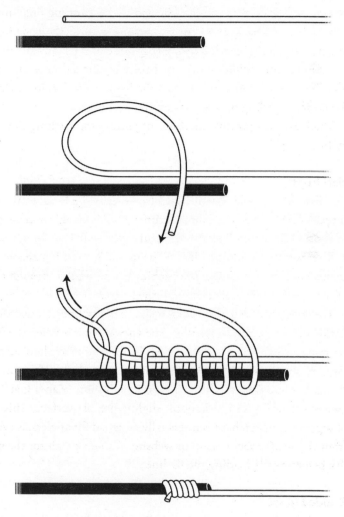

Fig. 7 – Nail knot – attaching backing or a leader to fly line

Fig. 8 – Tucked half-blood knot, used to tie fly to tippet

Braided nylon loops sometimes come with new fly lines or can be bought separately, usually in packets of ten. You can also buy kits to make up your own. They make simple, non-bulky and effective joints.

To fit a braided loop, 'sharpen' the end of the fly line by cutting across it at an angle and push the line up into the hollow braid towards the loop at its end. It can be awkward to do this as the end of the braid quickly starts to fray. The secret is to use the finger and thumb of both hands to ease the fly line inside the tube of the braid. It is important to get the end of the fly line right along to the loop to avoid a 'hinge' of empty braid. Once the fly line end is in place, trim off any frayed end of the braid. Pass a short length of nylon monofilament line or other thread through the braid loop as the means of pulling it through a short length of plastic tube provided to form a neat seal over the junction between the end of the braid and the fly line (see Figure 9).

EXTRA SECURITY

Some makers will tell you this joint is now secure. Most experienced fly fishers dispute this! They always complete this set-up by adding a drop of Zap-a-Gap superglue to both ends of the plastic tube over the junction.

You should take one additional precaution. Many big salmon have been lost, perhaps after being played for some time, when the braided loop has slid off the fly line despite the makers' claims of security and

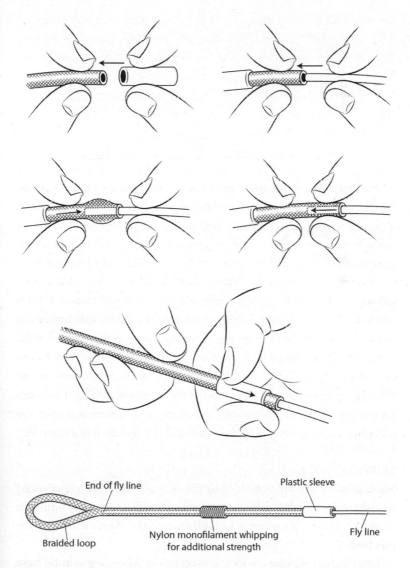

Fig. 9 – Braided loop and how to fit one, including additional whipping of fine monofilament

the application of superglue. Lay a length of nylon monofilament line of 2.7 to 3.1-kg breaking strain along the braid that covers the fly line. Place a needle alongside just as if you were tying a nail knot and whip nine or ten turns of the nylon over itself and the needle. Thread the end through the needle and pull it back under the coils. Pull both ends of the nylon to tighten it into a neat whipping. This will guarantee the braided loop is absolutely secure.

A 'tucked half-blood' knot (see Figure 8) is used to attach the backing line to the braided loop as shown. The tucked half-blood is the easiest and commonest fishing knot. It can be used whenever a line has to be attached to a 'loop' such as the eye of a hook, a swivel or a ring.

The end of the line is 'tucked' into the large loop formed when tying the knot to increase its strength. Get into the habit of doing this every time.

TAKING CARE WITH A NEW FLY LINE

Once the backing is joined to the end of the fly line, it can be wound onto the reel. The coils in the new fly line must be unwound carefully as the line is transferred from its plastic spool onto the reel. It may seem tempting to remove the new line from its take-apart spool, throw it onto the floor and then to wind it on to the reel. This is a mistake because it prevents the 'factory' coils in the new line being 'unwound' and puts permanent 'twists' into the line which you may never be able to get rid of.

Keep the fly line on its spool, put a pencil through its central hole, get a friend to hold it firmly and wind it onto your reel so that the coils are unwound carefully. As long as it is loaded onto the reel properly the first time, the fly line will, from then, always lie in 'natural' coils.

PLASTICISER

Some line manufacturers advise you to dress their new line with some liquid 'plasticiser' before it is used for the first time. Modern fly lines are impregnated with a plasticiser to make them slippery so that they 'shoot' further when cast. You pull the new line off the reel onto sheets of newspaper on the floor and then pull the line through a small piece of cloth soaked in the liquid plasticiser supplied. Leave it on the newspaper for an hour to dry before winding it back onto the reel.

It is wise to repeat this treatment every so often to clean the line and to replace the plasticiser which has leached out.

ATTACHING THE LEADER TO THE FLY LINE

Once the fly line is wound onto the reel, you have two choices. You attach a braided loop if you intend to use sinking poly-leaders. If not, a nylon monofilament or co-polymer leader has to be tied to the tip of the fly line. Inexperienced fly casters should use a tapered nylon leader as this will improve the 'turn over' of their casts. Good casters usually do not bother with this refinement and often use a three-metre level leader of 9-kg breaking-strain nylon and a one-metre 'tippet'. Nowadays many use expensive fluorocarbon line for tippets despite the fact that there is no evidence that salmon are 'line-shy'.

A nylon or co-polymer-tapered leader should be attached using a nail knot.

Nylon or co-polymer tightens securely over the fine tip of the fly line so an additional overhand knot at the end of the fly line is unnecessary. It still helps to smooth it over with Zap-a-Gap.

A nail knot is always the best option to join the thick butt of a tapered leader to the fly line because it provides the neatest join. If you put a braided loop on the end of the fly line, which may be supplied with it, any knot used to attach the thick leader end to the braided loop will be bulky and will tend to jam in the tip ring of the rod. Don't risk it!

USING A BRAIDED LOOP

Fitting a braided loop to the tip of the fly line (including the additional nylon whipping described above) provides a secure connection,

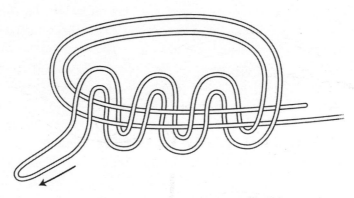

Fig. 10 – Three-turn loop knot and loop-to-loop knot

using a loop-to-loop knot (see Figure 10) for a poly-leader. They are supplied with a loop at both ends.

A level nylon leader can also be easily attached to a braided loop. Tie a loop at the end of the leader using a three-turn loop knot (see Figure 10) and attach this to the braided loop on the end of the fly line using a simple 'loop-to-loop' knot as shown.

Adding the final short nylon, co-polymer or fluorocarbon leader to the end of a sinking poly-leader should also be with a loop-to-loop knot.

JOINING NYLON OR FLUOROCARBON LINE

The best knot for joining two lengths of line is the 'full-blood' knot (see Figure 11). This is probably the commonest fisher's knot of all. It is neat and unobtrusive as well as being very strong. It is the knot you should use to join the end of a tapered leader to a short tippet.

KNOT-TYING HINTS

The full-blood knot is not the easiest knot to tie and it does take practice to tie it quickly and efficiently every time. There are special tools

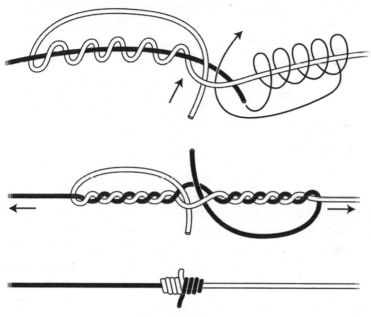

Fig. 11 – Full-blood knot

available to help you tie this knot if you cannot master it, but usually it is best to persevere. Practise using relatively thick monofilament nylon until your fingers and thumbs learn what to do.

Fluorocarbon line is notoriously difficult to knot. One reason for this is that it is not naturally stretchy or slippery and sometimes does not tighten easily. If this happens it can be 'thinned' and stretched by the knot-tying process. This severely weakens fluorocarbon. All knots should, therefore, be lubricated by spit before they are tightened and they should be closely examined afterwards. It is usually obvious if it has been 'thinned' or kinked. Reject such knots without fail and start again. Weak knots are the commonest cause of broken leaders and lost salmon!

PUTTING ROD AND REEL TOGETHER

All fly rods have a 'reel fitting' to accommodate the fly reel. Almost all modern rods have a screw fitting. This ensures that the reel seat can only be secured in the correct position on the rod so that the reel is in line with the 'butt ring', i.e. the first rod ring that the line will be fed through. The reel has to be the right way round i.e. positioned for left- or right-hand wind. You then need to thread the end of the leader through the reel line guard or the lower quadrant of the reel cage before threading it through the butt ring and then the 'intermediate rod rings' in turn.

Instead of struggling to thread the fine end of the leader through the rings, it is easier if you pull the leader off the reel and fold over the tip of the thicker fly line, threading the end of this loop of doubled line through the rod rings. Once the doubled fly line tip is through the 'tip ring', pull on the butt of the leader to get the rest of it through the rings.

TYING THE FLY ONTO THE LEADER

Once the leader is through the rod rings, the last task is to tie a fly onto the end of the tippet or leader. The commonest used, the tucked half-blood knot, has already been described above.

There is another knot that is also useful. This is the 'turle' and 'double-turle' (see Figure 12). The reason this knot is useful is that it tightens round the upturned eye of a salmon fly hook and gives better presentation of the fly without the 'hinge' that is inevitable if a blood knot is used.

A single-turle knot is used for small flies, size 10 and below, and finer tippets. If using flies of size 8 and above and 16.8 kg breaking-strain tippets or leaders, a double-turle is more secure. It may need plenty of lubrication (spit!) to bed down snugly.

Double-turle knot

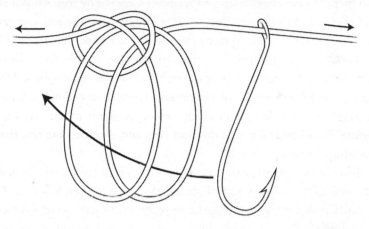

Single-turle knot

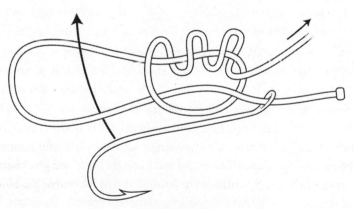

Fig. 12 – Single- and double-turle knots

OTHER WRINKLES AND SOME 'MUST-HAVE' TOOLS

A great joy of fly fishing is how little heavy gear you need. But that does not mean you need nothing other than your rod, reel, leader, flies and a landing net. There is a range of other bits and pieces that every fly fisher should carry. Not a day will pass when you will not be grateful you have got one or more of them. The following list will all fit into, or onto, the pockets of a fly fishing waistcoat.

Every fly fisher has a slightly different 'must-have' list. The purpose of this one is only to get you started! They're all available from every fly fishing shop or tackle dealer's website.

SPARE TACKLE

- A packet of braided loops – they may need replacing if lost or damaged.
- Fly boxes – two are probably enough, one for small flies and one for tube flies. Make sure they are small enough to fit in your pocket.
- Tapered nylon leaders. You might need one or two spares.
- Spools of nylon monofilament, co-polymer or fluorocarbon line for new leaders and tippets. The breaking strain should be matched to the size of the flies being used. You need 9-kg line for level leaders and for use with larger tube flies. Use 13.6-kg line if the river is full of sharp rocks and you expect big salmon. Use 6.8-kg breaking strain (or 9-kg with a 13.6-kg leader) for most tippets. Drop down to 5.4 kg when using size 10 or smaller flies.

STUFF

- A small piece of candle wax to prevent rod ferrules sticking.
- A felt pad and a small bottle of proprietary fly line plasticiser for cleaning a floating fly line that gets dirty.
- A small bottle of proprietary fly line de-greaser for cleaning a sinking line.
- A home-made paste of Fuller's Earth powder (available at any chemist's shop) and washing-up liquid to smear on nylon leaders to make them sink.

◆ A tube of Zap-a-Gap. The superglue specially made for anglers . . . you never know when you might need it!

TOOLS

◆ An engineered point to help open and untie the annoying over-hand knots that regularly appear in leaders and tippets. It is vital to remove these knots as soon as they occur because fluorocarbon, co-polymer and nylon lines are all greatly weakened when such knots tighten. A 'chunky' engineered point is easier to handle than a needle which does the same job.

◆ A thermometer. Salmon fishing tactics change as the water temperature increases.

◆ A proprietary hook-sharpening tool is a most essential piece of kit! Hook points blunted by use or turned over by contact with vegetation are a common cause of lost fish. The best tool is a thin stick covered in 'diamond dust' that fits inside a pen-like case. It costs about £8.

◆ A small pair of long-nosed pliers is essential to de-barb hooks. You just press the barb tightly to squeeze it into the hook. A de-barbed hook is a must if you intend to release the salmon you catch. A pair of pliers comes in useful for other jobs too.

◆ A Swiss Army Knife as no fly fisher can have too many tools!

◆ A Priest, the well-named tool that is used to knock a salmon on the head if you are going to take one home. They come in various shapes and sizes. You need a robust one to deal with a salmon. Prices vary depending on the material used. Anything is better than scrambling around to find a suitable stone or handy stick on the bank. Your quarry deserves a dignified end!

◆ A small pair of sharp-nosed scissors to trim flies or cut line. A good pair cost about £10.

◆ A pair of line snips is an even better way of cutting line and trimming the free end of line neatly after a knot has been tied. Most line snips also incorporate a needle point which is useful for poking excess varnish out of the hook-eye of a new fly.

◆ A small pair of surgeon's artery forceps is the fly fisher's tool of choice to reach into a salmon's mouth to retrieve a deeply swallowed fly. A salmon has sharp teeth which damage your fingers! Fishing tackle dealers sell them for around £5.

OTHER USEFUL AIDS

◆ Always carry a small 'rag' or, better, a packet of disinfectant wipes to keep your hands clean.

◆ A cheap pair of magnifying spectacles is very useful if you are over fifty years of age and have trouble focusing on anything within a few centimetres of your eyes! Grown men have been reduced to tears by their inability to thread line through a hook-eye in failing light. You can get a pair cheaply from any pharmacist or drug store.

◆ Polaroid sunglasses, including a cleaning cloth and strong case, are invaluable. They make a huge difference to your ability to see fish in the water by reducing glare. Getting them made to your prescription is a worthwhile investment. They also serve as eye protection when casting or fighting your way through the undergrowth.

◆ A few small, sealable plastic bags always end up being useful to carry some new-found treasure home. You can steal them from the kitchen.

◆ A 'bass' is essential if you are going to take a salmon home. They are made from a permeable material and keep a fish fresh if kept wet. Never put a salmon in a plastic sack . . . it will cook! A bass costs less than £5 or $5, unless you want a deluxe insulated version with a zip.

◆ A 'Fly Patch' is a useful means of carrying spare flies outside their box. You must not put a damp fly straight back into your fly box or the hook will go rusty. Fly patches with a lamb's wool lining which clip onto your waistcoat are the answer. It is much wiser to buy one that folds over to protect the stored flies than an open patch. A pretty leather one will cost around £15 or $15.

◈ If you are travelling around a fishery using your own car, you need Rod Carriers that will carry your rods on the vehicle. There is a range of designs using vacuum or magnetic anchoring. Do not travel too far using vacuum models without testing them regularly.

◈ A wader repair kit. A godsend when you need it.

'GIZMOS'

◈ Most fly fishers attach their snips and scissors to 'Zingers' or retractor strings which are pinned to their waistcoats. They allow you to use your tool on the end of the string, which retracts neatly when you have finished using it. They save you trying to remember which pocket it is in and, more importantly, from dropping it into the grass! A good-quality one which will not seize up the moment it gets wet costs about £7 or $7.

None of the above is essential, but they are missed when you forget them. Going fishing fully equipped marks one of the stepping stones from beginner to expert.

SUMMARY

◆ Assemble a fly rod by joining the tip sections first.

◆ Tape the joints of double-handed rods.

◆ Reverse a new fly reel to right-hand wind if you are left-handed.

◆ Match the fly reel to the line rating and 'fill' the reel with backing and line.

◆ Ensure the fly line and leader pass through the reel's line guard or the lower quadrant of the reel cage.

◆ Attach the backing to the reel spool using a Fisherman's Knot.

◆ Load a new fly line carefully onto the reel to 'unwind' its 'factory' coils.

◆ Join a tapered leader to the tip of a fly line using a nail knot. Coat it with Zap-a-Gap superglue.

◆ Put a braided loop on the tip of the fly line if you are using a level leader or sinking poly-leaders.

◆ Attach a 'tippet' to a leader using a full-blood knot.

◆ Tie a fly to the end of the tippet using a single- or double-turle knot.

◆ Tie on a hook used with a tube fly using a tucked half-blood knot.

◆ Everyone has a 'must-have' list of spares, stuff, tools and 'gizmos'. You should be able to carry them all in the pockets of your fly fisher's waistcoat.

EIGHT

USING A DOUBLE-HANDED FLY ROD

All professional fly casting coaches find that their easiest job is to teach an absolute beginner who has never fly fished before how to cast with a double-handed rod. The first reason for this is that the tip of a long rod moves a long way and its flexibility imparts the 'feel' of the fly line moving through the air that the new caster recognizes and responds to. The second is that the two-handed grip inhibits the instinctive desire to add 'back swing' to a cast and to 'break' the wrist to do so. This is an inevitable fault of a new caster using a light single-handed fly rod for the first time.

It is more difficult to teach an experienced fly fisher to use a double-handed rod for the first time. They assume a double-handed rod should be used just like a single-handed one and try to do all the work with their upper hand using their lower hand on the butt as a pivot for the moving rod. They have to learn that casting is a two-handed action and that the rod is held and cast at an angle across their body, not vertically like a single-hander.

But, in principle, the mechanics of casting are the same whether you cast with one hand or two. The purpose of this part of the book is to make you a competent caster no matter which rod you use. It assumes you have never cast any fly rod before. If you have, skip to the parts that help you.

HOW A FLY ROD WORKS

A springy, flexible fly rod and a thick, tapered line provide the force to propel a weightless fly over the water. Those who have studied elementary mechanics know that Force = Weight x Acceleration. The critical element in every cast is a flexing rod tip that 'accelerates to a stop'. The rod's acceleration and the weight of the moving fly line create the force of the cast. The 'stop' transfers all this into the unfurling line. Achieving the optimum force depends on maximizing the tensile strength of the flexing rod.

A catapult helps to understand what happens. Every schoolchild knows that when a catapult is loaded with a stone that is too light, even when the elastic is fully stretched, the stone will not go far. Conversely, if the stone is too heavy its weight will overwhelm the strength of the elastic and the stone will fall at their feet. But if the chosen stone is the 'right' weight, it will fly to its target. Fly rods and fly lines are sized, labelled and matched to be 'right' for each other when the 'head' of the 'weight forward' or Spey tapered line is being cast. The head of a standard 'weight forward' line used with a single-handed rod is usually nine metres or so long. The head of a Spey line used with double-handed fly rod is longer.

CASTING TECHNIQUES AND STYLES

This book describes three casts. The 'overhead cast' is used by most fly fishers most of the time. The 'roll cast' is used to get the fly line in position to begin an overhead cast but is sometimes a useful cast in its own right. You need to be competent at both casts to get started whether you are using a single- or double-handed rod. The third cast is the Spey cast. This is a cast that can only be made using a double-handed fly rod. It is an essential technique if you fish where there are trees behind you or a high bank that prevents the back cast of an overhead cast. It is an adapted roll cast. The long rod is used to sweep the line into the air before a roll cast directs it over the water. You must be able to execute both a 'single Spey' and a 'double Spey' cast. The choice of these casts is dictated by the direction of the wind and the river's current. They are not alternative ways of casting.

SINGLE-HANDED v. DOUBLE-HANDED RODS

Many European and UK trout anglers are put off having a go at salmon fly fishing because they listen to the traditional view that you cannot go salmon fishing unless you use a 'salmon' rod. This means a long, and expensive, double-handed fly rod. Conversely, most North American fly fishers who visit Alaska or Canada to fish for salmon pack only a single-handed #8 weight rod. They may have heard about double-handed fly rods but they have never thought of buying one. Who is right?

The pros and cons for each are listed below. One is not a better option than the other. In the end the choice should be dictated by the river you fish and the techniques it demands.

SINGLE-HANDED ROD

Advantages
- More accurate over short distances.
- Easier to retrieve line with the 'free' hand.
- Can 'double-haul' to aid longer casts.

Disadvantages
- Cannot Spey cast.
- May be difficult to lift back cast above bankside vegetation in some places.
- Does not handle big and/or weighted flies easily.

DOUBLE-HANDED ROD

Advantages
- Powerful. Can cast the right line a long way and makes 'roll casting' easier.
- Can handle big, heavy flies and may aid the use of sinking lines.
- A longer rod aids the control of a floating line as it is carried downstream e.g. by 'mending'.
- Essential if you need to Spey cast.
- Aids playing fish in big, fast-flowing rivers.

Disadvantages

◆ Difficult to short cast accurately and to retrieve line.

◆ May make landing and playing a fish more difficult in tight spaces.

◆ More difficult to transport.

In summary, the smaller the river the greater the advantage of a single-handed rod, but do not be put off having a go at salmon fly fishing for lack of a double-handed rod.

CASTING IN EASY STAGES

The casting 'lessons' that follow divide the technique required into easy stages for the overhead cast, the roll cast and the Spey casts.

You should treat them as a series of steps that need to be understood and mastered in turn before moving forward to the next. For each cast this progression, for those who have never tried to use a fly rod, may take an hour or more from beginning to end, but some star pupils move through faster. What everyone needs to establish is a practice routine that can be used again and again to build up confidence and competence. It is also a routine that you can return to later when you need to refresh your skills or to sharpen them, perhaps before moving on to a new technique or when trying out new tackle.

Fly casting confidently, especially in difficult conditions, can seem like a distant dream for many beginners when they first try. It can be even more difficult for those who have tried to get started without the help of a professional coach and who have become confused by the contradictory advice they receive. So, whether you are an absolute beginner or a befuddled 'improver', here is the very first thing that you should do before you start to practise the casts described in the next chapter.

The purpose of this exercise is simply to give you the confidence to use a fly rod and to trust your instincts.

The 'getting started' exercise

When learning to overhead cast for the first time, the best location is a large, unobstructed grass field before moving onto casting over water. Roll casting is best learnt over water from the start. No one can learn to fly cast when it is blowing a gale, so pick a day with light winds. If the wind is very light, face into the wind as this will help the 'back' casts you make. If the wind is stronger, and you are right-handed, face at right angles to the wind direction so that it is coming onto your left side. This wind will, helpfully, push the fly line away from your body when you try your first casts. Obviously, you should face in the opposite direction if you are left-handed.

Assemble your fly rod with the line and leader through the rod rings and tie a five-centimetre loop of wool on to the end of the leader tippet using a tucked half-blood knot. You need a fly or piece of wool on the end of the leader or else it will crack when you are practising. A piece of wool does not hook up in the grass.

Extend about two rod lengths (about three if using a double-handed rod) of fly line on the ground in a straight line from the rod tip.

If the rod is single-handed, grip the rod handle with your dominant hand so that your thumb is on top of the handle on the opposite side from the reel and pointing along the rod.

If the rod is double-handed, and your right hand is dominant, use it to grasp the rod handle above the reel and place your left hand around the rod butt. If you are left-handed reverse them so that your left hand is in the upper-hand position.

Your hands should be a comfortable distance apart, about the width of your shoulders. Clamp the line tight against the underside of the rod handle with your index finger.

A test

Now, without anyone telling you what to do, try this little test. Can you, using the rod, lift the extended line off the grass so that all the line is in the air and then can you put it back in exactly the same place and in the same straight line?

Don't worry if you cannot do it first time. Keep trying, walking backwards so that the line is straight out in front of you each time before trying again. Think of the rod as an extension of your arm or arms.

When you have taught yourself to do this, there is a second test. Can you now lift the extended line off the grass into the air and, moving the rod backwards and forward above your head, keep the line in the air without it dropping and touching the ground?

Timing

You will immediately realize the secret is in timing the backward and forward movements of the rod to let the line straighten out behind you and then in front. See if you can manage a couple of back and forward casts without stopping.

Try to pass these tests before reading any further!

Almost everyone can succeed in these two exercises just by responding to the 'feel' of the rod and line. You might like to imagine you are driving a coach and horses and you have been given a long whip that you need to use to gently touch the leading horses to encourage them.

If you have never tried fly casting before, you will 'feel' the cast more easily with a double-handed than single-handed rod. If you are an experienced single-handed caster and trying your first double-handed rod, you will be surprised by the slower 'timing' of the longer rod.

Two lessons

This exercise should quickly teach you the two fundamental lessons of successful fly casting. The first is that it is impossible to lay the line back down straight in front unless it has been allowed to extend out behind you in a straight line. You have to 'time' how long this takes before you move the rod forward.

The second is that you can only keep the line in the air if you ensure it extends fully in front of you and that it remains stretched tight by the moving rod once you have got it off the ground. If it goes slack, because of poor timing or hesitant backward and forward movements of the rod, you cannot stop the fly line falling to the ground in a heap! To start again you have to move backwards to straighten it.

Succeeding in these two basic exercises should give you all the confidence you need to learn to fly cast quickly. Do not worry if it feels difficult at first. It is like learning to ride a bicycle. You are very wobbly at first and then your 'muscle memory' kicks in and you cannot understand what was so difficult.

There is another parallel between bike riding and fly casting. Once you have learnt to do them, you never forget.

SUMMARY

◆ The critical element of all casting is a rod tip that 'accelerates to a stop'.

◆ All salmon fly fishers need to master both the 'overhead' cast and the 'roll' cast before they can fish effectively.

◆ Spey casting demands a double-handed fly rod. It is a technique used where there are trees or a high bank behind and the back cast of an 'overhead' cast is impossible.

◆ Choose a fly rod that suits the size of the river you are fishing.

◆ Tie five centimetres of wool to the end of the leaders when practising casting to prevent the line cracking like a whip.

◆ Use the simple 'Getting Started' exercise to develop 'timing' and the need to 'let the line straighten' between rod movements.

NINE

THE OVERHEAD CAST

An overhead cast is the cast most salmon fly fishers use most of the time, whether they are using a single- or double-handed rod. The mechanics of the cast are the same so using the rods is dealt with together in this chapter. Some differences in technique are highlighted.

The overhead cast is the cast of choice for salmon fly fishers wading well out into a river or who have no trees, tall vegetation or a high bank behind them preventing a back cast. If there are obstructions, a double-handed rod and 'Spey casting' is needed.

Nine- or ten-foot single-handed rods are matched with standard weight forward lines with tapered 'heads' that are about three rod lengths long.

Double-handed rods are matched with 'Spey lines' which have heads that are five rod lengths long or more. It is not a problem for the longer rods to cast and to control this length of line in the air.

If long casts are needed when using a single-handed rod, 'double-hauling' with a 'shooting head' joined to a finer 'shooting line' is often employed. This is not a different casting technique; it is simply the way to increase line acceleration during an overhead cast.

GRIP AND THE 'AT REST' POSITION

SINGLE-HANDED ROD

Hold the handle of a single-handed rod with your dominant hand so that the reel is below the handle and your thumb sits on top of the handle and points along the rod.

When 'at rest' and preparing to cast, your arm should be close to your body with your elbow bent so that the rod is horizontal and pointing where you wish to cast. You should feel comfortable.

DOUBLE-HANDED ROD

Hold the rod handle in front of the reel with your dominant hand, as with a single-handed rod. The other, lower, hand should grasp the butt of the rod behind the reel. When 'at rest', your hands should be a comfortable distance apart, about the width of your shoulders. If you are right-handed, the left arm should be hanging down alongside your body so that your left hand is beside your left hip. The rod should be horizontal; this means your right arm and hand, which should remain to the right of your body, have to reach forward to grip the rod (see Figure 13).

You should feel comfortable holding the rod this way. It means that the rod does not point straight in front of you. It points at an angle to your right. This 'at rest' stance is important. For all casts with a double-handed rod, this stance is the starting and finishing position. It should remind you that double-handed casting is a two-hand technique and the rod is cast backwards and forward slanted at an angle across your chest. Instinctively, those fly fishers used to a single-handed rod try to keep the rod vertical rod and end up with their lower hand over to the 'wrong' side of their body instead of pulling the lower hand back down to their hip when making a forward cast (see Figure 13).

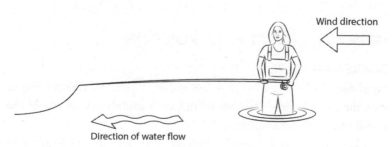

Fig. 13 – The start and 'at rest' position when using a double-handed fly rod with the right hand uppermost

STANCE

Face the direction of the cast. This may be easier to say than to do if you are wading deep in a fast-flowing stream and struggling to keep your feet. However, it is worthwhile to take the time to adjust your feet so that you face directly where you are aiming, whether it is at right angles across the steam or more downstream. Get stable. Nothing ruins a cast more than losing your feet during its execution.

Remember when you are at the 'at rest' starting position using a double-handed rod and facing where you are aiming, the rod will not point in that direction.

You cast with your arm(s), not your whole body. A firm stance helps keep your body and head still. This is what makes your casting look elegant.

BREAKING DOWN THE CAST

An overhead cast can be broken down into four elements – the 'back cast', the 'forward cast', 'false casts' and 'shooting line'.

The back cast is the most important. Overall, the technique depends on the initial execution of the back cast.

The following steps describe this casting sequence. Learn each one before moving on to the next. The sequence is also a practice routine and each element can be practised separately. Following the routine helps you understand common faults and problems. You can return to it in order to provide correction and reassurance.

You cannot watch yourself casting. This is why a coach helps. Some casting coaches resort to movie cameras, but it is also a great help to learn in a group and to watch other fly fishers. Seeing what others do reinforces everyone's knowledge of good technique and the universal faults!

THE RULES!

Before you attempt any overhead cast, it is vital to understand there are three rules that must always be obeyed. Not heeding, or even understanding, these rules is a common cause of frustration, even among experienced fly fishers.

They are:

◆ An overhead cast cannot begin unless the fly line is extended straight out from the rod tip and is on the surface of the water. In a river the current helps to do this. It eventually pulls the line directly downstream of the caster.

◆ The cast should start with the rod held horizontally in front of the caster, who faces in the direction of the cast.

◆ Throughout the initial back cast and all the subsequent forward and back casts, the rod's movements should be in the same plane i.e. the rod should not move backwards in one direction and aim forward in another. This means that, in a river, the rod will have to be moved horizontally to point across the river. The direction of the fly line pulled downstream by the current should be ignored.

STAGE ONE

THE BACK CAST

The best place for a first lesson in overhead casting is a large, open field. The space enables you to walk backwards to ensure the line is extended straight out in front before attempting each new back cast.

Take account of the wind

Before you start, choose the direction you will cast so that any wind is blowing the line away from your body, i.e. from left to right if you are right-handed. Face in this direction.

Pull line from the reel and walk backwards so that around eight or nine metres of line (i.e. approximately three rod lengths, most of the coloured 'head' of a two-colour line) is extended on the ground straight in front of you. If using a double-handed rod, you should extend three or four metres more.

Grip

Hold the rod comfortably with your dominant hand. All fingers should grasp around the handle with the thumb along the top (the opposite side to the rod rings) and pointing to the rod tip. You can control the fly line by passing it over your hooked index finger below the cork handle of the rod. Your finger acts like an extra rod ring directing the line onto the reel. More importantly, it provides instant control when you need to hold the line tight against the rod handle during casting and fishing. Your other hand, which also has to grasp the butt of the rod when using a double-handed rod, is used to hold and to retrieve the line when casting and fishing.

Hold the fly line tightly against the cork handle with your index finger. The rod should be horizontal. Your hand(s) will be around waist level. Now, try your first back cast.

Single-handed

If using a single-handed rod, concentrate on your casting arm. Use your forearm only, with wrist stiff, to move the rod tip in a smooth, accelerating ninety-degree arc. Watch the rod tip. The rod should come to a sudden stop when it is pointing vertically upwards. The rod handle should be close to your ear. The critical motion is a final 'accelerate and stop', timed as a short, precise 'power arc' over the last quarter of this cast.

Double-handed

When using a double-handed rod, the movement is essentially the same but both arms are used to move the rod at an angle across your chest so that when it comes to a stop it is canted over at a narrow angle (about ten degrees) from the vertical. The lower hand will be below your chin and the reel will be level with your ear (see Figure 14).

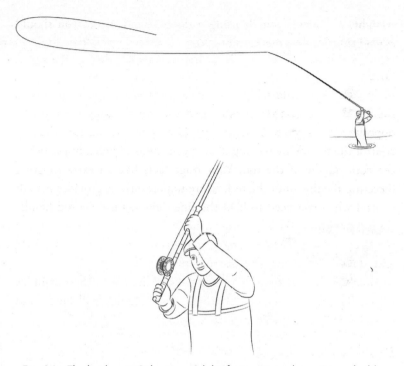

Fig. 14 – The back cast. Side view and the facing view when using a double-handed rod

At first, forget about casting forward. Let the line fall behind you. The big field allows you to reposition yourself for the next attempt. Get the back cast right before moving on to the next element. This takes practice! You will not get it right first time.

Start slowly!

At first everyone tries to move the rod tip too fast, too soon. Start slowly! The rod tip, especially when using a double-handed rod, has a long distance to travel. It must be at maximum acceleration when you stop. Achieve maximum velocity too soon and the rate of acceleration will be zero during the critical 'power arc'. Elegant casters look unhurried!

Aim high

It also helps to imagine you are aiming to extend the line behind you above a three-metre hedge. This should not be difficult. The rod is already adding three metres or more to your own height!

You will know you have got the back cast right when you feel the rod flexing backwards when the fly line has unfurled completely behind you. Soon, you will feel this 'pull' every time, especially when using a powerful double-handed rod. It helps if someone watches and encourages you. A qualified coach will get you there in a few minutes!

STAGE TWO

THE FORWARD CAST

The pull of the extended line flexing the rod backwards is the signal for the forward cast. The forward cast requires little effort after an effective back cast. After all, the tensile strength in the flexed rod straightens it and starts the forward cast even if you do nothing. Only a short, accelerating 'power arc' to another sudden stop is needed, so that the rod stops at about forty-five degrees. Then, a gentle follow through to bring the rod back to its horizontal, starting position.

When using a double-handed rod, the lower hand has to move down and backwards to get back to the 'at rest' starting position with the lower hand by your hip.

The aim is to ensure the line unfurls in a tight loop so that it fully straightens out in the air before the lowering rod helps to drop it gently onto the water or grass.

Do not try another cast at this stage. Just concentrate on achieving one strong back cast that results in a perfect forward cast which lays the line straight out in front.

STAGE THREE

FALSE CASTS

Using a single-handed rod

Everyone struggles to get started on a new cast. The reason for this is simple. The optimum length of fly line you need beyond the tip ring is the eight- or nine-metre head of a WF line. Getting this amount of line out in front is easy on a field where you can walk backwards, but this is not an option at the waterside.

False casts are required. The purpose of a false cast is to keep the fly line in the air in order to extend the optimum length of line beyond the rod tip before a final 'delivery' cast is made.

It's difficult. There is not enough weight of fly line beyond the rod tip to make the fly rod flex properly and to transfer its power to the extending line. This 'getting started' stage is when everyone suffers from tangles and other minor disasters.

You cannot start an overhead cast by pulling lots of line through the rod tip so that it lies in a heap in the water. The line must be extended in front of you before you can start an overhead cast. One way of doing this is to use a roll cast, which is described in the next chapter, but mostly fly fishers extend the right length of fly line through the rod tip by making a couple of false casts.

Similarly, when you are fishing, you may want to retrieve your fly close to you before you re-cast, and this will mean you will only have two metres or so of fly line beyond the rod tip. This too needs to be extended by false casting.

The practice exercise

To practise false casts, start as if you were practising a back cast. The eight- to nine-metre head of the fly line should be extended in front of you on the grass or in the water. Use your 'free' hand, the left if you are right-handed, and, keeping the rod horizontal, pull about four metres of the fly line through the rod rings so that it lies in loose coils at your feet. Keep hold of the line with this hand. Use the index finger of your other hand, which is holding the rod, to control the retrieval of this line and to ease out any kinks or tangles.

Aim high

When you back cast now you will notice that the 'pull' of a good back cast is weak because there is so little fly line beyond the rod tip. Let the line straighten behind you as before and make a forward cast aimed at the tops of some distant trees. Imagine them if necessary! 'Accelerate to a stop' until the rod is about sixty degrees above the horizontal. As the fly line unfurls in front of you, lift your index finger to release the line and 'open' the fingers of your other hand. The line will begin to move through the rod rings. A perfect false cast should take most of the eight- to nine-metre head through the tip ring. Use the light friction created by both hands to keep the moving line 'tight'. Before the line stops moving through the rod rings, clamp the line to the rod handle with your finger and commence a new back cast. This back cast will be easier than before because the whole eight- to nine-metre head is the 'right' weight to load the rod.

Never release line through your fingers on the back cast

You should only release the line on the forward cast where you can see it moving and can gauge the strength in the cast. You must always clamp the line with your index finger if the moving line is 'running out of steam' before it slackens.

Aim to keep false casting to a minimum. Even the most expert caster struggles to maintain their timing for more than three or four false casts.

The less fly line there is through the rod tip, the more difficult it is to false cast. Always start a new overhead cast with as much fly line as possible beyond the rod tip.

Three-cast rhythm

Develop the habit of using one false cast to get the 'feel' of the line in the air, another to extend the line's head and then a final 'delivery' forward cast. Stick with this three-cast rhythm, even if the false casts are not perfect. This helps develop the 'muscle memory' to repeat this rhythm without thinking about it.

If a cast goes wrong, stop. Let the line fall and start again.

There is nothing elegant about lots of false casts used in an effort to extend a fly line!

USING A DOUBLE-HANDED ROD

Happily, there is less need for false casting if you are using a powerful double-handed rod.

The 'standard' overhead cast is to retrieve the fly line until most of the 'head' of a Spey or WF line extends beyond the rod tip, and is stretched tight by the current, and then to cast it in the required direction with a single overhead cast.

The maximum change of direction that can be made easily with a single cast is about sixty degrees (see Figure 15).

A GREATER CHANGE IN DIRECTION

Occasionally, your fly line may be extended straight downstream by the current and you want to cast directly across the river. Instead of attempting a ninety-degree change in direction, it is easier to make a single false cast about forty-five degrees downstream and then a final delivery cast in the desired direction. Remember to move your feet to face the direction of each cast.

This technique can be practised on a field.

GETTING THE LINE ONTO THE SURFACE

A double-handed rod can only lift the whole head of a fly line off the surface of the water.

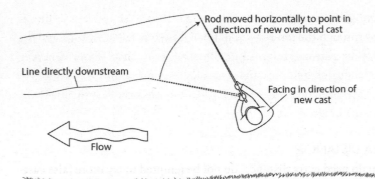

Fig. 15 – Cast in the required direction. Ignore the direction of the extended line

There is no problem if using a floating line. But you will break your rod if you try and lift a sinking line which is below the surface. Even a floating line to which a long, fast-sinking tip has been attached can be impossible to lift to the surface. You have to retrieve most of these lines before a new cast can be made and, even then, a roll cast (see Chapter 10) may still be needed to get it onto the surface.

STAGE FOUR

SHOOTING LINE

The final stage of the overhead cast exercise is to 'shoot' line with the final delivery cast. After a good back and forward cast, you will have felt the pull from the line unfurling in front of you. To lengthen your cast all you have to do is to properly time letting this line go so that it 'shoots' out as the final forward delivery cast is completed. Timing is vital! If you let go too early, the unfurling line will sag and the cast will collapse. Ideally, the pull of the forward cast should trigger your fingers to let go.

AIM HIGH

Do not aim for the water's surface. By aiming for a point about two metres above the water, you establish the right 'muscle memory' to achieve good turn over above the water, then a 'shoot' as the line is pulled through the rod rings and, finally, a gentle fall of the line and fly.

Aim for a strong, but measured, delivery cast that shoots about the same length of line on every cast. There is no point in straining to cast to the horizon every time. Settle for a comfortable and consistent distance.

EXTRA DISTANCE?

If you do need extra distance, do not be tempted to try more false casts or to extend more than the fly line head beyond the rod tip. Instead, put a little more effort into both parts of the final delivery cast. More line acceleration in both the backward and forward casts and consistent timing is all that is necessary. This is something you normally keep in reserve.

If you are using a single-handed rod it is possible to use the 'double-haul' technique to squeeze even more distance out of the overhead cast, especially if you are using a shooting head line.

THE DOUBLE HAUL

The technique of 'hauling' is easy to describe but it does take a little practice. It is used only with single-handed rods because it makes use of the free hand to manipulate the line.

The force of an overhead cast, and its distance, depend on the line's acceleration during the 'power arc' of the backward and forward casts. When your casting is perfect and you cannot move the rod tip any faster, the only way to increase line acceleration is to pull or 'haul' the line with your free hand. But to be effective, your timing must be spot-on! This is what takes practice.

SINGLE HAUL FIRST

Begin by trying to haul only as line acceleration peaks during the back cast. This is a 'single haul'. Do not try to do it when making the forward cast until this single haul has been perfected. You will feel this. The rod will flex more as the back cast is completed, the line will stretch tight behind you and the forward cast will be more powerful. As this builds your confidence, introduce a second haul to the power arc of the forward cast. Get it right and you will be amazed by the increase in the strength of your cast (see Figure 16).

Three clever adjustments to your overhead cast help to double haul. These are:

◆ If you are right-handed, move your left foot half a pace forward and cant the rod away from the vertical. 'Hauling' is easier if you watch the rod tip, and this is easier if it is out to the side. If there are no obstructions, it can even be horizontal.

◆ Throughout the cast, hold the line in your left hand very close to your right hand and follow the rod's movement with this hand to maintain this position. This can be awkward to do at first if you have never thought about the position of your 'free' hand before.

◆ Make short 'hauls' of approximately 30 cm. The commonest fault when hauling is to make long pulls. Timing the short hauls correctly is what is critical. After each short haul during the back cast, allow your hand to be 'pulled back' close to the butt ring so that you are ready to make the second haul on the forward cast.

COMMON FAULTS

It takes a little longer to become a perfect caster if you teach yourself than if you are working with a coach.

Counter-intuitive

It takes time to master the basics. Try not to get frustrated. Fly casting is counter-intuitive. Your head tells you all the effort should go into the forward cast because that is where you are aiming! But because a

Fig. 16 – The double haul cast

fly rod uses its tensile strength to transfer its power to the fly line, a good back cast loads the flexing rod and the forward cast almost takes care of itself.

The commonest casting fault you will see is fly fishers straining for a stronger forward cast but failing, and often not even trying, to deliver a powerful back cast. Without this back cast, their overhead cast will always be a struggle.

'Weak' wrists

There is a common myth that some fly fishers using single-handed rods have weak wrists and that their wrists 'break' as they cast, thus spoiling their overhead casts. They are even persuaded to buy devices to wear on their wrists which attach to the rod butt and act as a 'splint'. They need no such help!

What they are doing is executing perfectly good back casts, but, after the 'accelerate-to-a-stop' power arc, they fail to hold the rod absolutely still before starting their forward cast. Instinctively, they treat the rod, like a tennis racquet or a bat and, unconsciously, seek 'back swing' to increase the power of the forward cast. The effect is catastrophic! The tension in both the flexing rod and the extending line is instantly lost. The source of power for the forward cast has gone.

This is also a common fault by those using double-handed rods. There cannot be a 'break' between the hands, but novice casters are tempted to seek back swing and move the rod backwards instead of holding it still before starting their forward cast.

This is what a good coach prevents from the outset. Unfortunately, there are fly fishers who have been struggling to cast well for years, and who have never sought help, and who just do not realize what they are doing wrong. Cruelly, the harder they try, the worse they get! They put in even more backswing in a futile effort to beef up their forward cast!

Tailing loops

The other common fault that needs to be avoided is a 'tailing loop'. This occurs when the leader and fly at the end of the fly line cross the body of the line during the backward or forward casts, creating the risk of tangling. 'Tailing loops' are caused by poor timing of the application of power during the short power arcs, such as starting the forward stroke too early before the line is fully extended behind.

The same problem can also be caused by jerky movement of the rod tip. Only practice will 'smooth' the rate of line acceleration and the 'timing' of the 'power arcs'. Get them both right and the result is elegant casting...your ultimate aim!

DEALING WITH THE WIND

Wind direction and its effect on the line in the air is a critical factor in effective overhead casting. If there is a head (or facing) wind, the 'power arc' of the back cast should tilt forward into the wind to create a high back cast with a lower forward 'stop' and follow through. The aim is to shoot the line 'below' the wind. The power arc itself should not become longer.

If there is a following wind from behind, the opposite applies! The power arc should tilt backwards from normal, delivering a low back cast if obstructions permit. Then a high forward cast and a high 'stop'. Aiming into the sky takes advantage of the wind and aids a gentle delivery.

Single-handed rods

A cross-wind which takes the fly line in the air away from your body is welcome as long as it is not too strong. A cross-wind in the other direction is a curse!

On lakes you will usually see one bank has been deserted by right-handed fly fishers when there is a right-to-left wind blowing along it. It makes casting difficult as the line in the air is blown into your body whenever your timing is less than perfect. On a salmon river you do not usually have the luxury of changing banks to suit the wind direction!

Backhand

There are two simple solutions. The first is to practise to cast with a backhand style. If you are right-handed, you angle the rod to your left and cast over your left shoulder. This puts the fly line in the air to the left, and downwind, of your body.

Ambidextrous

The second option is to learn to cast left-handed (or right-handed). This sounds like an awesome prospect to most people. In practice, it is actually remarkably easy to become an ambidextrous caster. It is not the timing of the casting that you will struggle with, it is getting the fingers of your 'wrong' hand to hold and to manipulate the fly line comfortably.

Do persevere; it is a great skill to master and will serve you for a lifetime!

Double-handed rods

Change hands

The greatest advantage of fly fishing with a double-handed rod is that you can change the side of your body on which you overhead cast just by swapping your hands. If you have your right hand uppermost on the handle and the left at the butt, you cast over your right shoulder and vice versa.

So, if using a double-handed rod, no matter which direction the wind is blowing along the river, you can cast on the downwind side of your body so that the wind takes the line in the air safely away from you.

Commonest fault

It is exceptionally difficult to fish with a double-handed rod on the 'wrong' side of your body on a very windy day (not uncommon on northern salmon rivers!), but, amazingly, this is the commonest fault seen and the inevitable reason why many struggle with double-handed casting. It is a particular problem for those who come to try salmon fly fishing and to use double-handed rods after a lifetime of single-handed fly casting.

'I am right-handed,' they insist. 'I cannot ever learn to cast a fly rod with my left hand uppermost! And they refuse to try.

This is in sharp contrast with the beginner who has never fly fished before. They have no problem with learning to cast over both shoulders and quickly appreciate the immense advantage of being able to adjust instantly to the vagaries of the wind. They can also go on to learn to roll cast and spey cast where it is obligatory to fish over your downwind shoulder (see Figure 18).

CHANGING THE DIRECTION OF A CAST

The salmon fly fisher usually fishes a 'downstream and across' style. You cast across the river and the line drifts downstream with the current. Because you are stationary, and acting as a pivot, the moving line pulls the fly behind it, giving the impression it is 'swimming' across the river until the line is stretched out directly downstream. So, to re-cast back across the river demands a significant change of direction.

Fortunately, the overhead cast allows for easy changes in the direction of the cast of up to sixty degrees, but it is common to see fly fishers getting this wrong. They fail to obey the rule that both the backward and forward casts must be in the same plane.

Another common fault

It is a common fault when changing direction to make a back cast in the direction of the extended line and then a forward cast in the new direction sought. This creates a large, unwieldy loop. The fly or leader usually tangles with the body of the line as it unfurls.

Instead, make sure you move your feet to face in the correct direction, keep the rod tip low and sweep it slowly sideways to point in the direction required before lifting the straight line (always essential) off the water and casting normally (see Figure 15). Ignore the direction the line has been pulled by the current!

If you require a really wide change of direction, you should use one or two separate false casts, moving the feet and rod tip to face the new direction with each cast.

The critical rule of overhead casting is that the rod must stay in the same vertical plane for each backward and forward cast.

SUMMARY

OVERHEAD CASTING: THE 'RULES'

◆ An overhead cast cannot begin unless the fly line is extended straight out from the caster and is on the surface of the water.

◆ The cast should start with the rod held horizontally in front of the caster.

◆ During the initial back cast and all the subsequent forward and back casts, the rod's movements should be in the same plane i.e. the rod should NOT move backwards in one direction and aim forward in another.

THE BACK CAST

◆ Start with the rod held horizontally.

◆ A single-handed rod is an extension of the forearm, so keep the wrist stiff.

◆ Start slowly! Watch the rod tip.

◆ Smoothly accelerate to a stop.

THE FORWARD CAST

- Keep your hand absolutely still after completing the back cast.
- Wait until you feel the extended line flexing the rod.
- Do not move your hand backwards!
- Cast forward smoothly; accelerate to a stop at forty-five degrees.

FALSE CASTS WITH A SINGLE-HANDED ROD

- Ensure the line to be 'shot' is in loose coils and not tangled.
- Aim the forward cast at a point six metres above the water.
- Do not release the line too early.
- Clamp the shooting line with your index finger before it stops.
- Get into a three-cast rhythm.

SHOOTING LINE

- Do not let go too early when releasing the line.
- Aim for a point well above the water surface.
- Aim for a comfortable distance. Do not strain for a long cast each time.

HINTS WHEN USING A SINGLE-HANDED ROD

- Try rotating the rod to the right (if right-handed) by nearly ninety degrees to place the reel behind the wrist. This 'feel' of the reel helps to prevent 'back swing'.
- Alternatively, (if right-handed) move the thumb a little to the left from the top of the rod and point the index finger along the right side of the handle. The wrist is stiffened by an extended finger.
- Grip the rod more tightly just before the 'stop' position is reached. This helps to achieve the sudden stop required and to hold this position until you start the forward cast!

◆ Cast by lifting the forearm directly in front of your nose to prevent the back cast going beyond the vertical.

HINTS WHEN USING A DOUBLE-HANDED ROD

◆ The start and finish position for each cast is the hands on their own side of your body. This means the rod will be pointing at a slight angle to the direction of the cast.

◆ The rod is angled across your chest when you cast. Do not try to keep it vertical.

◆ Do not push your arms forward when casting. Keep your hands close to your body and move your bottom hand down and backwards to the start position during the forward cast.

◆ You MUST swap the position of your hands over on the rod handle so that you always cast over the shoulder that is on the downwind side of your body.

FINALLY GETTING IT RIGHT!

◆ The line lifts from the water without disturbance (if it is splashy, the initial acceleration is too fast and needs to be slower and smoother).

◆ The line unfurls in a tight loop over the top of the rod.

◆ You have 'muscle memory', perfect timing and a three-cast false casting rhythm if you are using a single-handed rod. You'll never forget how it's done!

TEN

THE ROLL CAST

The overhead cast is the cast that most salmon fishers use most of the time, whether they use a single-handed or double-handed rod, but there is another cast they must learn . . . the roll cast.

The first rule of overhead casting is that the fly line must be straight out in front before the cast can start.

When the fly line is first pulled off the reel it will fall in loose coils below the rod tip. A roll cast is the 'getting started' cast. A roll cast lifts this loose line into the air and, with a single forward movement, casts it out straight in front on the water.

Now, the overhead cast can begin.

There are other occasions when a roll cast is necessary. For example, if a cast goes wrong, the fly line will end up in a mess on the water. It has to be straightened out before the next overhead cast. Or, a sunk-line has to be lifted out of the water and laid out straight on the surface before it can be cast again.

The aspiring salmon fisher will read and hear a lot about fly casting and various fancy casts. But, at first, there are only three casts – the overhead, the roll and the Spey cast (which is an adapted roll cast) – that must be in every salmon fly fisher's armoury.

It pays to learn to do them well. Understanding how and why they work prevents endless frustration later.

For some, skilful fly casting becomes a passion. For the rest, it is simply the means to an end. Being able to cast accurately and in all weather conditions is the start of learning to fly fish. Nobody ever caught a salmon while casting. How the fly is 'presented' after it is in or on the water is what counts!

Do not become obsessed with casting. Understanding your quarry is more important than being able to exhibit the use of the tools!

WHY IS THE ROLL CAST IMPORTANT?

Learning to roll cast is essential. If the fly line is not extended out in front of you it is fatal to attempt an overhead cast! You must do a roll cast to extend it. The roll cast is not the easiest cast because there is no powerful back cast and a flexing rod to aid the forward cast.

In practice, the salmon fly angler has less need to roll cast than the still-water fly fisher because the running water often straightens out a wayward line, but sometimes it is the only way to position the line for the next overhead cast. There is another valuable use for the roll cast. It gets a line out when there are obstructions behind. The fly line hardly goes behind you when you roll cast.

The roll cast must be practised over water, not on a field. Pick a spot where there is plenty of room around you and a minimum of vegetation to catch the line. A small, low jetty is ideal. Although salmon fly fishers cast into running water, it is wise to practise roll casting for the first time on a lake or pond or over still water.

STANCE AND GRIP

Keep your feet close together. Face the direction you are going to cast. Hold a single-handed rod well up the handle, thumb on top. If using a double-handed rod, your two hands should be a comfortable distance apart, about the width of your shoulders.

Before you try a first cast, pull line off the reel so that it lies close to your feet. Then, hold the rod point very close to the surface of the water in front of you and waggle it. The effect of the surface tension 'holding' the line enables you to get seven or eight metres (a few more if using a double-handed rod) of line on to the water in front of you safely and easily. To extend these loose coils out into a straight line in front of you a roll cast is needed.

Later you will be able to roll cast the whole head of a weight forward or Spey line, but do not start with too much to do.

Check the wind! You must have a crosswind that takes the line away from your body. A left-to-right crosswind is essential if you are right-handed and using a single-handed rod. Do not attempt your first roll cast if there is a crosswind in the opposite direction!

If you are using a double-handed rod you must cast over your down-wind shoulder. If that is your right shoulder, your right hand is the 'upper' hand in front of the reel and your left hand will grasp the butt. These hands must be swapped over to cast over your left shoulder.

By far the commonest casting problem you will see on a salmon river is fishers attempting to use a double-handed rod on the wrong side of their body because they insist they can only cast over their right shoulder. They are wrong! An hour's practice would solve their problem. And it is quite impossible to roll or Spey cast effectively or safely if the wind is blowing the fly line towards your body!

MECHANICS

The roll cast is a two-stage cast. The first is lifting the loose coils of fly line into a large loop beside you by raising the rod. The line forms a capital 'D', of which the rod is the straight line. The tip of the fly line must remain in the water. The second stage is the 'power arc' to roll the 'D' loop through the air in the desired direction.

STAGE ONE

The lift
While you carefully watch the end of the fly line in the water, lift the rod up so that the reel is close to your ear and the rod tip is pointing backwards thirty degrees beyond the vertical. Cant the rod over a little away from your body. The line will follow the movement of the rod tip. Wait for the end of the fly line to stop moving. This tells you the 'D-loop' is fully formed.

You can now see what this 'lift' has done. The tapered tip of the fly line is in the water to the downwind side of your body, creating an 'anchor' that will help tension the line. The belly of the line is hanging from the rod tip to form a 'D-loop' to provide weight. The roll cast depends upon a precise 'power arc' from this standing start.

STAGE TWO

The power arc

The cast is a short forward movement which moves the rod tip from thirty degrees behind the vertical to thirty degrees in front. Once again, this cast is 'accelerate to a stop'. To ensure the maximum rate of acceleration at the 'stop', it is vital to start slowly. It is much better to sacrifice some final acceleration rather than to move so fast initially that the rod is no longer accelerating when you suddenly stop. The result is a loop of line rolling forward well above the water which then drops gently to the surface (see Figure 17).

This roll cast 'power arc' takes practice! The movement is higher up than an overhead cast, but it still depends on rapid acceleration from a slow start and a downward rather than forward movement.

DOUBLE-HANDED IS EASIER

This cast is easier with a double-handed rod. The rod is longer, so the 'D-loop' created is bigger. The two-handed movement, with the lower hand on the butt of the rod moving down and backwards to its starting position beside your hip, is more powerful. Practise this cast. You need to be good at it to become a competent Spey caster (see Figure 18).

WIND

You must take account of the impact of the wind.

'Easy' wind

If you are using a single-handed rod and are right-handed, the 'easiest' wind is one that comes from your left-hand side. The reason is

Fig. 17 – The roll cast with a single-handed rod

obvious. This wind keeps the fly line, including the rolling loop as the cast is made, away from the body so that there is no danger of being struck by the fly. The 'anchor', where the tip of the fly line is on the surface of the water, has to be in line with your body or to the right.

Fig. 18 – The roll cast with a double-handed rod. Adjusting hands to cope with the wind

Keeping the line to the right is the reason the rod is canted over a little towards the right before the power is applied to make the cast.

Difficult wind

If the wind is coming from the right, a roll cast must not be made on the right-hand side of the body. If you tried to roll cast in such a wind, both the 'D-loop' and the rolling loop would be blown into your body as the cast is made and an untidy tangle is inevitable.

There is a solution. You have to form the 'anchor point' and the 'D-loop' on the left-hand, downwind side of the body. If you are using a double-handed rod you simply swap your hands over and cast over your left shoulder. If you are using a single-handed rod you can also swap hands and cast with your left hand. It is surprising how easy it is for most of us to do this.

Backhanded

Alternatively, if you are a determinedly right-handed caster, you have to cast 'backhanded' over your left shoulder, keeping the single-handed rod in your right hand. The hand position, and the application of power, must be just the same as if the cast were on the right. It takes a bit of practice.

Wind from behind

If the wind is coming from directly behind, its effect is to collapse the 'D-loop', thus reducing the 'weight' available to make the cast. To counter this, as the lift is made, the rod tip has to make an exaggerated movement backwards into the wind to get into a start position closer to the horizontal than usual. The cast should be made the moment the fly line tip stops moving before the wind further collapses the 'D-loop'.

Aim high

The secret of making this cast is to ensure that, although the 'power arc' starts further back, it remains as short and precise as before. The effect is to aim the cast high. You will find the following wind aids and will smooth out the delivery after the essential sudden 'stop' as you lower the rod tip gently to the water's surface.

Facing wind

A facing wind from directly in front creates the opposite problem and mirror-image solutions. The facing wind tends to increase the 'D-loop' but then to collapse the rolling loop when the cast is made and to blow it back into your face. Counter this by not pointing the rod as far backwards at the start of the cast. The wind will ensure the 'D-loop' is formed. In effect, the starting point for the 'power arc' has been moved forward. The arc the rod tip follows should still be through sixty degrees to a sudden stop, but the effect is to drive the rolling loop forwards and downwards as if you are aiming to force it under the wind. This does work!

CHANGE OF DIRECTION

A weakness of the roll cast, in contrast to the overhead cast, is that large changes in direction cannot be made.

This is a constant problem in running water as the fly line is always being stretched downstream by the current. You can face downstream and roll cast the line in approximately the same direction. But you cannot turn to face in another direction and then roll cast across the stream. If you try, all you will succeed in doing is lifting the line painfully into your face.

Advantage of a double-handed rod

Such a change in direction can only be completed successfully when, before you lift the rod into position to form the 'D-loop' beside you, the anchoring line tip and leader are directly in front of you or are on the same side of your body.

This is what a Spey cast does! And it is why many salmon fly fishers use a double-handed rod.

If you are limited to a single-handed rod in a fast stream with obstructions behind you, it may be possible to make a series of small changes in direction by moving the line upstream with exaggerated movements of the rod tip to get it in front of you, but you will inevitably be defeated by the current. It is wiser to give up and return with a double-handed or Switch rod. Do not get frustrated by attempting the impossible.

THE JUMP ROLL CAST

The double-handed or Switch rod enables you to Spey cast when obstructions behind you prevent an overhead cast. This technique is described in the next chapter.

Another cast, the jump roll, is used by salmon fly fishers occasionally when fishing down narrow, fast streams with obstructions behind. This cast is easier if you are using a double-handed rod because of its length, but you can just about get away with it when using a shorter rod.

The purpose of the cast is to defeat the effect of a fast-flowing stream on a normal roll cast. If you have such a stream in front of you it prevents the essential 'D-loop' forming as you lift the rod into position by sweeping the line downstream.

The jump roll works because you make the extended line 'jump' from the surface as you move the rod into position to roll cast, so that the line comes towards you far enough to form a 'D-loop' beside you as the tip of the line splashes back down (see Figure 19).

TIMING

The secret of this cast is to start with the rod horizontal, to lift the line off the surface by rapid, upward acceleration of the rod tip and then to slow down as the rod passes the vertical to stop at the starting position about thirty degrees behind. The line tip should fall back onto the water surface a couple of metres in front of you to create the essential

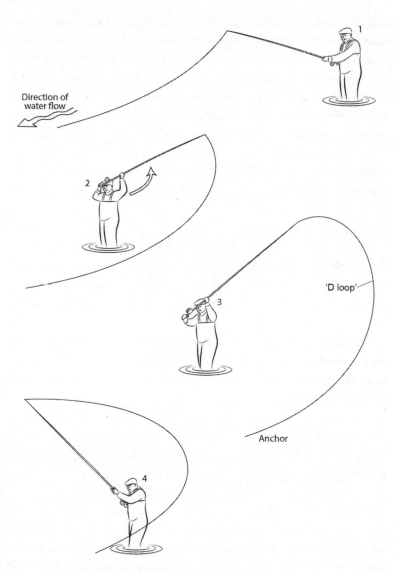

Direction of water flow

'D loop'

Anchor

Fig. 19 – Jump roll cast with a double-handed rod

anchor point. You make the roll cast as soon as you see the line splash down before it is swept downstream again.

Getting the timing correct for this cast is easier than you might think because you can see what is happening and adjust to get it right.

This cast can be particularly useful when your fly is covering a narrow stream or when you need to lift a sunk line to the surface before it begins to sink further into 'dead' water. It cannot be used to make anything more than a minimal change in direction (say about twenty degrees) of the extended line. A greater change in direction demands a Spey cast.

SUMMARY

◆ The roll cast is essential to straighten out a line which is loosely coiled beyond the rod tip before an overhead cast can be made. Every fly caster must be able to roll cast.

ROLL CAST – THE RULES!

◆ A roll cast must be made on the downwind side of your body.

◆ Lift the rod so that the reel is level with your ear and the rod tip is pointing upwards and behind you at about thirty degrees from vertical.

◆ Wait until the 'D-loop' is fully formed by watching for the tip of the line to stop moving.

◆ Start slowly! Accelerate-to-a-stop when the rod is in front of you at about thirty degrees from vertical i.e. a movement through sixty degrees.

ROLL CAST – HINTS THAT HELP

◆ Always aim at a point a metre or so above the water as an aid to improving/shortening the 'power arc'.

◆ There will be a length of fly line beyond the rod tip which is the optimum distance to roll cast because it is long enough to create an 'anchor' point and to provide enough weight in the 'D-loop' to flex the rod. Practise with this length, marking the line if necessary, before trying to roll cast further.

◆ A good roll caster is able to 'shoot' line by releasing it as the rod 'stops' and the line rolls out.

◆ It is much easier to use a double-handed rod and a Spey cast to change the direction of the extended line than it is to make a series of roll casts with a single-handed rod.

◆ A 'jump roll' is the way to ensure a good 'D-loop' when the line is in a fast-flowing stream.

If new casters practise hard, their casting skills will rapidly improve as their 'muscle memory' kicks in. It is like learning to ride a bicycle and will never be lost. If this does not happen, there is something fundamentally wrong with your technique and you need to consult a qualified angling coach.

ELEVEN

THE SPEY CAST

You cannot fly fish for salmon until you can cast. However, casting prowess does not make you a successful fisher. Many people obsessed by casting cloak the skill with an air of mystery and magic. Spey casting, especially, receives this treatment. Ignore it!

Spey casting is easy.

If you learn to Spey cast for the first time, as many do, on a lake or pond, you need to take time to refine your newly acquired skills in the place you really need them . . . a fast-flowing salmon pool. You do need to understand how the cast works and the effect of the wind to adjust as you wade down a river of changing depth and flow.

The emergence, in the last few years, of fly lines specifically designed to aid Spey casting is a great boon. They are made with various lengths of weight forward heads. Choose one that matches your rod length and your competence.

Like all casting skills, Spey casting is like riding a bike. Once you've got it, you will never forget how to do it.

The aim of this chapter is to get you there as quickly as possible. You can then concentrate on the more important task of learning how to fly fish for salmon.

WHAT IS A SPEY CAST?

The two Spey casts are known as the 'single' and the 'double' Spey. Both are modified roll casts. They are complementary elements of a single technique, not different casts. They are described together in this chapter. The salmon fly angler must master both.

Whether you use a single or double Spey depends upon the direction of the river's current, the bank you are fishing from and the direction of the wind.

A Spey cast is used instead of an overhead cast in those situations where there are obstructions such as trees or a high bank behind you that would foul the back cast of an overhead cast. The final 'delivery' element of a Spey cast is a roll cast. The line does not travel far behind you.

The casting style was developed on Scotland's River Spey, which is tree-lined for much of its length.

As explained in Chapter Ten, a roll cast must form the essential 'D-loop' on the downwind side of your body. The tip of the fly line has to be in the water in front or downwind of you. If you try to roll cast on your up-wind side, the fly line will be blown against you or into your face. This is dangerous!

Similarly, if the fly line has been stretched out downstream of you by the river's current . . . and it usually is . . . an attempt to roll cast across the river will only succeed in lifting the line into your face.

Unlike the overhead cast, where you can ignore the position of the extended line and cast back across the river, a roll cast has to be in the same direction as the extended line.

The Spey cast, essentially, is the means of moving the fly line into a position in front of and beside you, to allow a final roll cast in the direction you desire.

ESSENTIAL, NOT BETTER!

Some salmon fly fishers get into the habit of Spey casting all the time. Usually this is because their overhead casting technique is so poor that they are constantly clipping the stones on the bank behind them and breaking the points off the hook(s). They would be wiser to brush up on their casting skills because there are occasions where the precision and accuracy that can only be achieved by an overhead cast are essential.

SPEY FLY LINES

Modern 'Spey' fly lines have been specifically developed to aid Spey and roll casting. They have a weight forward profile that incorporates a long tapered tip and thicker, heavier belly at the rear of the head section before it tapers back into the thinner 'shooting' line (see Figure 3).

'Spey' lines are made in various combinations of the 'length' and 'weight' of their weight forward heads. You must match the weight (e.g. #9–10) to the rods' 'rating'. This ensures you can maximize the rod's power when the whole of the line's head is extended beyond the rod tip. You choose the length of head. The longer the head the bigger the 'D-loop' that has to be formed to execute the final roll cast.

In practice, if you are using a relatively short double-handed rod of twelve feet or so, and have no need to cast a long way, it is easier to use a 'Spey' line which has a 'short' head (around fifty feet). A longer rod of thirteen to fifteen feet makes it easier to form a bigger 'D-loop' and cast further. Even novice Spey casters should be able to manage a 'medium' head (around sixty-two feet). The Spey lines with the longest heads (around seventy-three feet) need skilful handling to maximize their capacity to create large 'D-loops' and to cast long distances using long rods (see Figure 20).

They are best left to expert casters.

STANCE

To Spey cast you must face the direction of the cast. This can be more difficult than it sounds. If you are wading in a fast-flowing stream and struggle to stay upright as you try to move a couple of steps between each cast over uneven, slippery stones, it is difficult to find a firm foothold. It is better to take the time to do this than to try to cast when you are unstable and facing wrongly.

In some places where the stream is narrow you will want to cast directly across the stream at right angles to the bank. In other places

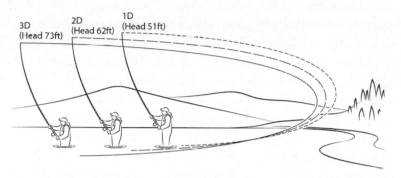

Fig. 20 – The 'D-loops' formed when casting with Spey lines with different head lengths

the correct cast may be more downstream. This is one reason why it is best, if you can, to wade out into the river so that you are in flowing water. This straightens out the line directly below you and holds it tight as you manoeuvre and get a firm foothold before you cast. There is more on the art of wading in Chapter 13.

WIND AND RIVER FLOW

The final 'delivery' element of a Spey cast is a roll cast made on the downwind side of your body. The river's flow dictates the position of the extended line downstream of the caster at the start of each new cast. So, if you are Spey casting from the left-hand bank of a river (looking downstream) with the flow from right to left and an upstream wind from left to right, the 'delivery' roll cast has to be on the upstream, right-hand side of your body. This is achieved by a 'single' Spey cast. If the wind is in the opposite direction i.e. right to left and downstream, then the final roll cast has to be on the downstream, left-hand side of your body, which demands a 'double' Spey cast.

Thus, the most important 'rule' of Spey casting is that, if the wind and the river's flow are in the same direction, a double Spey cast is required; if they are in opposite directions, it is a single Spey cast.

As emphasised in the previous chapters on casting, the wind dictates the side of the body on which the cast is made and the positions of the hands on a double-handed rod. Your right hand is uppermost on the rod and your left hand is at the butt if your right side is downwind. Your left hand is 'up' if the wind is in the opposite direction.

It does not matter whether the cast is a single or double Spey, it is the wind direction alone that determines the position of the hands.

Breaking down the Spey casts

Spey casts consist of three elements – the lift, the sweep and the final roll cast. The following steps describe this casting sequence for both the 'single' and 'double' Spey casts. It is vital to understand what each element of the cast is aiming to achieve so that making the necessary adjustments becomes automatic as you wade in deeper or shallower water or the strength or direction of the river's current change.

The easiest way to learn the rod movements required to Spey cast is to imagine that you have a large blackboard in front of you and chalk attached to the rod tip. All you have to do is to concentrate on the movement of the rod tip to 'draw' the lines described below.

THE RULES

◆ The fly line and leader must be straightened out by the current before the cast can commence. If it is not, because of turbulence or still 'dead' water, use a roll cast to straighten it out.

◆ The length of fly line extended beyond the rod tip should be the same for every cast. Experiment to find the optimum length, normally the 'head' portion of the line that maximizes the rod's power. Modern Spey lines usually change colour at the junction of the 'head' and 'running line' and provide a marker for judging this optimum length. Retrieve line to this length before each cast.

- Face the direction you intend to cast, not downstream.
- If the river's flow and the wind direction are the same, a double Spey cast is required. Then, the final element, the roll cast, is on the downwind side of your body.
- If the river flow and wind are in opposite directions, a single Spey cast is required, for the same reason.
- The position of the hands on the double-handed rod is determined by the wind and therefore which side of the body the cast is made; if the right side is downwind the right hand is uppermost, and vice versa.

STAGE ONE – THE LIFT

Before you start a Spey cast, the optimum length of fly line should be straightened out by the current downstream of you, and your feet should be firmly grounded and pointing in the direction you wish to cast. Now swivel slightly at the waist to point the rod down the extended line and, keeping the chalk and blackboard in mind, lift the rod tip to 'draw' a vertical line.

The purpose is to 'lift' the belly of the line off the water's surface so that only the tip and leader are still in the water and they are on the surface. The profile of the weight forward heads of 'Spey lines' helps because their bulk is concentrated at the rear of the head.

The height of this lift is dependent on a number of factors. If the current is powerful, it pushes the tip of the fly line to the surface even if a sinking line or poly-leader is being used. In a slower current, more height is required to get both the bulk of the head into the air and the tip to the surface.

If you are using a floating line and no sinking poly-leader, you can make the lift and delay the rest of the cast indefinitely. This cannot be done if you are using a sinking line or poly-leader because it immediately starts to sink again if there is a delay. In fact, a fast-sinking line or one of the latest 'super-fast-sinking' poly-leaders can make Spey casting almost impossible because the line and/or its tip sink too quickly to be raised to the surface by the 'lift'.

The only solution is to retrieve some line, lift the rod high and make a careful roll cast along the direction of the line and, as soon as the line touches the surface, to move smoothly and instantly into the lift.

STAGE TWO – THE SWEEP

Single Spey

The purpose of the second element of a Spey cast is to get the fly line into the air and positioned to enable the formation of a perfect 'D-loop' on the up-wind side of your body. If the wind is blowing upstream, a single Spey is required. The 'sweep' is simple! Remember the imaginary blackboard and chalk on the rod tip.

You have already drawn a vertical line with the lift. Now make a right angle and draw a long horizontal line along the blackboard until the rod tip is pointing upstream. The 'secret' of a successful sweep is smooth acceleration to a stop. The sweep does not have to be fast! If you start slowly and deliberately, it is easier to keep accelerating. The surface tension of the water and the strong current will hold onto the line tip on the surface, the rod will flex strongly and the whole line will be launched strongly into the air as the sweep continues to accelerate.

You have completed the sweep when you have 'drawn' half a rectangle on the imaginary blackboard and when you stop moving the rod tip horizontally (see Figure 21).

Double Spey cast

If the river's flow and the wind are in the same direction, a double Spey cast is required. The purpose of the 'sweep' is the same as for

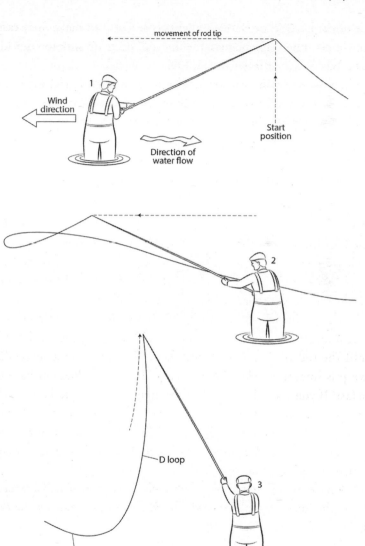

Fig. 21 – The 'lift', 'sweep' and delivery roll cast of a single Spey cast

a single Spey. The sweep has to get the fly line into the air and positioned to enable the formation of a good 'D-loop' for the final roll cast. But this final roll cast must be made on the downwind and downstream side of the body, so the sweep is longer and more complicated. It can also be disrupted by the flow and currents in the river. But it is still simple.

The imaginary chalk and blackboard are a great help. Concentrate on the movement of the rod tip! The first half of a double Spey cast is exactly the same as a single Spey. 'Lift' vertically to get most of the head of the line off the water and the tip to the surface. Draw a right angle and long horizontal line until the rod tip is pointing upstream. Ensure this long movement starts slowly and then accelerates to a stop. This lifts the line into the air and throws a loop of line upstream. The rod tip should now 'draw' another right angle and move vertically downwards to the water surface. Just before the tip touches the surface, 'draw' a third right angle and then draw a long horizontal line just above water. In effect, the rod tip 'draws' a complete rectangle and the rod tip is back where it started (see Figure 22).

The purpose of completing the rectangle is to get the body of the Spey line and its tip back in front of you and ready to be lifted safely into a 'D-loop' on the downwind side of your body. These rod tip movements should be smooth and deliberate. Do not try to move the rod as fast as you can.

STAGE THREE – THE 'DELIVERY' ROLL CAST

When the sweep is completed, whether it is a single or double Spey cast, the rod now has to be lifted into position on the downwind side of the body to make the final roll cast.

Single Spey

As you complete the horizontal sweep of a single Spey, the fly line loses momentum as the rod is moved into position for the roll cast. The heavy rear portion of the Spey line's head follows the rod's movement to form the essential 'D-loop'. By the time the rod is perfectly positioned, the tip of the fly line will be falling onto the water to create the 'anchor' point for the final roll cast. If the cast has been perfect, the tip of the moving line will 'kiss' the surface of the water about three metres upstream from where you are standing.

This is the signal to start the 'delivery' roll cast of the single Spey (see Figure 21).

Double Spey

As you end the long horizontal sweep back to the starting point of a double Spey and raise the rod into position for the final 'delivery' roll cast, the fly line's movement through the surface throws a characteristic spume of water into the air. When this surface disturbance stops, it is the signal that the 'D-loop' will not get bigger and it is time to complete the roll cast (see Figure 22).

GENERAL – SINGLE AND DOUBLE SPEY

Although it helps to differentiate the mechanics and the purpose of the three elements of the Spey casts, they work best when performed as a one, uninterrupted movement.

A smooth lift from the end of the 'sweep' into position to perform the final 'delivery' roll cast keeps the line moving through the air and enhances the formation of the essential 'D-loop' on your downwind side. This line movement, along with the tip of the line's contact with the water surface, provides the 'anchor' that flexes the rod and provides 'beef' for the final delivery.

Get to the right position

So, do not compromise on getting the rod into the right position to make the roll cast. The rod should be lifted up until the reel is at the level of your ear. Height increases the size of the 'D-loop'. It should

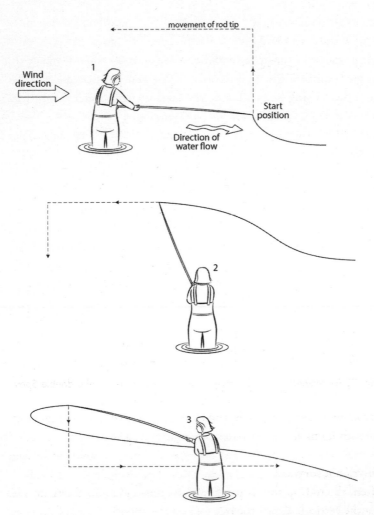

Fig. 22 – The 'lift', 'sweep' and delivery roll cast of a double Spey cast

be pushed back so that it is at an angle of about thirty degrees beyond the vertical and canted away from you to keep the rolling line clear of your body. This allows the final delivery roll cast to start slowly and

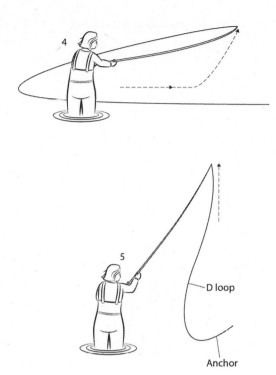

Fig. 22 (continued) – The 'lift', 'sweep' and delivery roll cast of a double Spey cast

accelerate to a stop through a final 'power arc' that aims the line high and rolls it out above the water (see Figures 21 and 22).

Down, not forward

Often, the rod tip travels too far. It should stop about thirty degrees past the vertical. Aim at the tree tops on the opposite bank of the river. Remember, the roll cast should be aimed in the direction you choose. The rod should be moved down, not pushed forward, so that the lower hand on the butt ends up beside your hip.

If a Spey cast is good, you will be able to shoot line by lifting your index finger and letting it go as the cast is completed and the line unfurls above the water. Do not let go too early or it will ruin the final delivery.

You will find it easier to shoot line and to achieve extra distance with the single Spey cast.

COMMON FAULTS

Despite understanding the mechanics, some beginners still find Spey casting difficult. They need to understand what they are getting wrong. If they don't, it really helps to spend an hour or two with a licensed coach.

The commonest problems are:

- Many fly fishers, especially if they do lots of casting with single-handed fly rods, struggle with swapping the position of their hands on a double-handed rod so that they can cast properly on the downwind side of their body. They say, 'I am right-handed', and insist on having their right hand uppermost on the rod at all times. This means that they can only cast properly (no matter which cast they choose) when their right is the downwind side of their body.

- The same anglers often fail to make both hands move and work the rod. Their upper (right) hand dominates. They try to cast as if they are using a single-handed rod. They keep it too upright and their bottom left hand does not work hard enough, often failing to help push the rod tip down and backwards as it moves back to its final position beside their hip at the end of each cast.

- Perhaps the commonest reason of all for poor Spey casts is failing to use the imaginary chalk tip and blackboard advice. It is vital to 'draw' the half rectangle when doing a single Spey and to point the rod tip upstream before lifting into position for the final roll cast. Most beginners are in too much of a hurry to lift into the roll cast position.

◆ Similarly, when doing a double Spey, the temptation is to 'draw' a square rather than a rectangle due to over-eagerness to get into the roll cast position. This haste is fatal. Line acceleration through the air is poor and the essential large 'D-loop' is not formed.

All these faults are corrected by using the trick of 'drawing' on an imaginary blackboard and concentrating on the movement of the rod tip. Get the rod tip's path right and the line will follow it. If the movement is also smooth and accelerates when necessary, the cast will be spot-on! Practice makes perfect.

TOP TIPS

SPEY CASTING – THE RULES

◆ Spey casts are completed by a final, 'delivery' roll cast which must be made on the downwind side of the body.

◆ The hand on the downwind side must be the upper hand on the double-handed rod.

◆ The single and double Spey casts are not options. When the flow of the river and the wind are in the same direction, you employ a double Spey. If they are in opposite directions, a single Spey.

◆ Ensure a firm foothold, facing the direction of the cast.

◆ The fly line beyond the rod tip should be pulled straight by the flow of the river before the cast starts. Wade out into the flow if necessary.

◆ The length of fly line extended beyond the rod tip should provide the optimum weight to use the power of the rod (usually the coloured head of a 'Spey' fly line). Retrieve or release line to use the same length for each cast.

HINTS THAT HELP: GENERAL

◆ Use a modern 'Spey' weight forward line with a short or medium head. Leave long heads to the experts.

◆ Start every cast with the rod horizontal and pointing down the extended line. This means twisting your waist a little.

◆ Imagine that your rod is tipped with chalk and there is a blackboard in front of you. Concentrate on the rod tip and the lines you 'draw'.

◆ Spey casts have three elements: a 'lift', the 'sweep' and a final 'delivery' roll cast. Although they should form a smooth, uninterrupted whole, necessary adjustments are easier if you understand what each stage does.

◆ Good roll casting technique is essential. This is the element of Spey casting that can be practised separately. Do it!

◆ The purpose of the 'lift' is to get the body of the fly line into the air and the tip of the line onto the surface. Spey casts will not work if the line or tip has sunk. If it has, you need to do a careful roll cast to put the line on the surface and then instantly start the 'lift'.

◆ Lifting the rod high to perform the final roll cast increases the size of the 'D-loop' and the effectiveness of the casts.

◆ Aim high in the air, not at the water.

HINTS THAT HELP – SINGLE SPEY

◆ The initial 'lift' is vertical and the 'sweep' is a long horizontal movement of the rod tip. In effect, you 'draw' half a rectangle.

◆ The 'sweep' should accelerate to a stop. It is easier to maintain the necessary acceleration if you start slowly.

◆ The commonest fault is lifting into position for the final roll cast too early. Continue the horizontal 'sweep' until the rod tip is pointing upstream.

HINTS THAT HELP – DOUBLE SPEY

◆ For this cast the path of the rod tip is a continuation of the single Spey. In effect, the rod tip 'draws' the complete rectangle.

◆ The second half of the 'sweep' and lifting the fly line into the roll cast position cause a characteristic disturbance on the water surface. Wait until it stops; this means the 'D-loop' is fully formed, before making the final delivery cast.

◆ Do not be overambitious about the distance you can achieve at first.

TWELVE

WHERE AND WHEN TO FISH

Any book on salmon fishing can tell you where in the world to go fishing. By examining accurate catch records it is also easy to advise on prime time and the most prolific beats. It is more difficult to identify the best pools, runs and streams in a chosen beat or river and even harder to say what time of day is best or when conditions will be favourable. Every river is different!

Listen to your guide or ghillie or any other local angler. Experience is the key. Salmon choose the same 'lies' and are caught in the same places and at the same times year after year. Fortunately, there are some general rules that help. This chapter makes sense of them.

'DEAD' WATER, 'LIVE' WATER AND THE 'TAKING STRIP'

The character of salmon rivers varies enormously. The behaviour of their populations of salmon depends upon the conditions, such as the water height and the time of year. It can be hard to decide where to wet your line. The good news is that much of any river can be ignored. The salmon fisher must learn to recognize the 'live' stretches of the river. The rest of the river is 'dead' and should be ignored.

Even within well-known pools and runs, salmon crowd into the most comfortable and safest areas i.e. the 'live' part. These change as conditions change. A rising river will move them to 'high water lies', probably in the same pool, before they return when the river drops.

In short, the first step in 'reading' any pool or stream is to divide it into the 'live' and 'dead' sections. Then you have to work out how to position yourself so that you can achieve perfect fly presentation in the 'live' sections.

'DEAD' WATER

Salmon pass through 'dead' water but their aim is to find a comfortable and secure 'lie'. This may be a place where they rest, very temporarily, or where they may stay for a long time. 'Dead' water is too fast or too slow, too shallow or too deep, too turbulent or too placid for salmon to find a comfortable lie.

'LIVE' WATER

'Live' water is where all salmon 'lies' are found. 'Live' water is more difficult to describe. It may be a metre-wide depression in the bed of an otherwise inhospitable stretch of water, but, more usually, lies are in bigger pools or steady streams where salmon find a 'comfortable' flow and a depth that offers security.

Salmon seek out a flow where they have to use some effort to hold station in the current, but are rewarded by the oxygen exchange provided by the water movement through their gills. Salmon fly fishers recognize 'live' water. It is where the current's strength gives good fly presentation.

'Live' water may not be deeper than a metre or so, but there is usually some deeper water nearby that offers more security. This is where a hooked salmon in a shallow stream will always run to.

In *Salmon Fishing*, Hugh Falkus went further. He introduced the concept of the 'taking strip', a narrower section of the stream in 'live' water where fly presentation was best and where you were most likely to hook a fish. The great value of this idea is to emphasize the importance of perfect fly presentation over the likeliest spot.

The pools, runs and streams where running salmon congregate are usually well recognized. As long as their character is not changed by winter floods or ice, the same places provide comfort and security to salmon year after year.

There are also places within such pools which may be particularly attractive. Here's why.

'Creases'

A 'crease' is the boundary between flowing water that is too fast or too turbulent to make a comfortable, permanent lie for a salmon and water that is also not comfortable because it is too slow or too shallow. It is usually a precise boundary and thus a narrow strip of water. An obvious 'crease' is described in Chapter 15 in the neck of Quillachan Pool on Scotland's Findhorn River where the rapids at the head of the pool meet a cliff and the river has cut a deep stream as it changes direction. This narrow neck, which salmon seem to visit frequently in low water, is too fast for them to lie there permanently but they do lie in the 'crease' at its edge. This is the 'taking strip' in this part of the pool. This is where your fly should tarry and be worked through carefully.

There are other 'creases' in many pools. Sometimes the water is forced through narrow gaps between rocks or hard against one bank. Often this creates fast water bordered by slow, with an obvious, narrow 'crease' between them. Concentrate on getting fly presentation right here. Adjust your wading path and plan accordingly.

A 'gentler' stream

The heads of many salmon pools are rapids. Perhaps it is a torrent down a steep rocky or gravel slope, or even down a waterfall into deep water, but the result is often turbulent and foaming white water. Salmon may be seen leaping here, making their way upstream through this strong stream, but in low water, when they are reluctant to run, the fish may only be visiting for a welcome 'hit' of highly oxygenated water. They are caught here, but only occasionally.

Salmon are much more likely to be caught on a fly at the point where this maelstrom gathers itself and becomes a 'gentler' stream. Here, it straightens out but a strong flow remains. The lack of turbulence seems to make it much more comfortable for lying salmon, even in high water when they may be queueing up to face the rapids ahead.

It could even be the 'lead' position for a shoal of salmon that are competing for space and comfortable lies in a crowded pool.

The reason does not matter. But if you are wading down a salmon pool, this 'gentler' stream is often the best chance of finding a 'vulnerable' salmon in the whole pool.

Ridges, outcrops and 'croys'

Salmon pools and streams are not usually uniform stretches of water. More often, the flow is disturbed by ridges rising from the bottom or outcrops pushing out from the bank. In Scotland, an outcrop from the bank is often called a 'croy' and they are often man-made additions. They 'squeeze' the flow of water through the pool. It speeds up, changes direction and deepens beyond or alongside the obstruction. This creates a lie for salmon. Time and again, this is where a 'vulnerable' salmon is found.

In a pool where it is obvious that fish are running through and some are resting for a time, you can almost guarantee they will rise to your fly beside or just beyond such an obstruction that has quickened up the stream.

Rocks and boulders

Some salmon pools and streams where fish lie run over a flat gravel bed or rock. Favourite lies are not obvious. Pools where the river bed is littered with underwater rocks or boulders are different because these obstructions in the stream often act as a magnet to salmon lying in the pool. Perhaps such rocks provide some protection for the fish from predators.

Underwater rocks and boulders are usually revealed by the turbulence they create on the surface as the flowing water is forced around and over them.

Salmon lie a metre or two in front of these rocks or beside them where the current speeds up. They never lie in the turbulent water behind them. Even if the rock or boulder reaches above the surface, you cover most fish as you fish your fly in front of it before your fly can snag on it. However, the 'best' boulders are those that are small enough and deep enough to be fished over with most fly lines or sinking poly-tips but big enough to cause some obvious surface turbulence.

Again, these obstructions are the place in a pool where running fish seem to rest and become 'vulnerable'.

The upslope at the tail of a pool

All salmon pools and streams become shallower as they come to an end. Often there is a long gentle upslope before the smooth flow breaks down into rapids as the river falls more rapidly towards the next pool. Lying salmon often prefer to lie on this upslope, especially if it is steep in a short, deep pool. As the pool becomes shallower, the flow increases. Perhaps this is what makes this section of the pool more comfortable for lying salmon. If attacked, they are not far from the deeper water in the body of the pool. The water flow accelerating towards the tail also helps the presentation of a fly cast across it. The tail of a pool is also an obvious temporary resting place for a running fish which may just have fought its way through many kilometres of rapids below. They often reveal their presence with a tempting 'head-and-tail' rise. Never ignore this! Such fish are especially 'vulnerable' to a well-presented fly.

THE IMPORTANCE OF WATER HEIGHT

The critical factor

Although the features detailed above are attractive to salmon looking for a lie, none is as important as the height of the water. In some rivers the impact of the river's level may not be as important as that described in Chapter 15 for Quillachan Pool where 'dead' water becomes 'live' water as the level rises, but rising or falling water moves salmon to different lies in all rivers as they seek comfort and security. It also changes their 'vulnerability'.

This is why, if you are being aided by a guide or ghillie, their advice on where to fish will depend on the height of the water and whether it is rising or falling. They will know from experience which pools fish best at a particular height and whether any of the features above come into play. Act on this advice.

Unproductive lies

This knowledge can pose a particular dilemma for ghillies on some Scottish rivers where a high number of rods share a beat, or on any other rivers where fly fishers 'compete' for the most likely stretches of the river and the best pools.

For example, there are some pools where fish lie and regularly reveal their presence by leaping but where they are very rarely caught. The reason may be that good fly presentation is extremely difficult at most water levels.

Sometimes there is a particular height of water when all this changes and the fish become 'vulnerable'. In practice, this should be the only water height when a ghillie should advise one of his clients to fish this pool, but if space is in short supply and the fisher usually sees a fish or two, it will probably be fished every day.

If you are a client, it is wise to question ghillies about when and how often fish are caught from each pool. They will usually tell you if you press them!

'Vulnerable' lies

Similarly, a good guide or ghillie will know that there are places in specific pools or stretches where salmon, whether resident or resting, become particularly vulnerable at certain water heights. If he has several clients, they cannot all fish over these 'hot spots' at the same time. To share them out as fairly as possible, the ghillie should air his dilemma and let his clients decide for themselves.

High water

In general, a river that is high has more potential lies where a resting or resident salmon can find comfort and security. It opens up more water for the fly fisher to explore. Falling atmospheric pressure that heralds an incoming depression and its accompanying rain seems to trigger 'vulnerability'. And when the rain comes, and the river first rises, the water remains clear for a time before it becomes dirty and muddy. This 'window' of higher, clean water can offer a short but magical chance.

Fish through again and again

High water gets salmon on the move, both new fish running in from the sea and those that are forging further upstream. This means a lie can be unoccupied one minute and holding a resting fish the next. There are some lies where travelling fish seem to be so vulnerable that the wise tactic is to fish through them again and again.

Follow running fish

Alternatively, it is sometimes possible to target a pod of salmon moving slowly through a stretch of river in high water and to follow them from pool to pool.

Be observant. React to what you see. Salmon usually reveal their presence.

A clearing river

Most rivers that are unusually high will begin to fall back to normal levels when the rain stops. A falling, clearing river is always more productive than a rising river that is getting more dirty by the minute. However, as the river falls, the salmon have to find new lies and move back into, or find, the holding pools that will be their home until the next flood. The successful fly fisher is the one that chooses the best places to fish and selects new flies as the level drops.

If you have a guide or ghillie, they will tell you where and how. Listen and learn.

KEEPING A RECORD

If you do not have help identifying the different 'hot spots' as the river falls, it is more difficult. Choose the pools and places where salmon are showing, if they are, and look out for the features listed above.

If you are a regular visitor (or intend to return), the most important thing is to keep a record of any salmon you (or anyone else) catches or loses, where it was hooked, the size and pattern of the successful fly and the exact height of the water. This is where you should get another one when the river is that height next time.

Over time, such accurate records are invaluable. Every fly fisher's memory is notoriously unreliable.

A SINGLE-MINDED APPROACH?

There are no salmon fly fishing competitions. For most salmon fishers, who do not fish on the most prolific and exclusive rivers at prime time, catching a salmon is quite an achievement. Getting two or three would make it a red-letter day.

This is why you should be single-minded and ruthless, especially when conditions are in your favour. Who does not need the sense of achievement that comes with having a 'big' day to balance the blank days every salmon fisher suffers?

WHAT DOES 'SINGLE-MINDED' MEAN?

Start with the conditions. Is the river too low, too high, or is it a 'perfect' height? Is the weather too bright, too wet so the river is rising, or is it a cloudy, mellow day that all fly fishers welcome?

In all conditions there are some tactics that should give you an edge. Employ them.

Low water

For example, if the river is low, the weather is hot and bright and the fish have been uncooperative for days, you should fish early and late and concentrate on the streams, pools and places that experience tells you do occasionally give up a salmon in low water. The chances are that there are very few 'vulnerable' fish in the river, so it makes sense to be the first one to fish down any likely pool if you can manage it.

Salmon in some pools may be making 'visits' from their normal lies to sport themselves in the fast water at the neck of a pool. Target them there, focusing on the crease between the fast and slower flow where they may take a few minutes' rest.

Perfect water

On the other hand, if conditions are 'perfect', perhaps fining down gently after a flood that has brought in fresh fish, you should make a plan to take full advantage of your luck. Start at dawn and finish at dusk. The longer you fish, the more you will catch.

There will be many more 'vulnerable' fish than usual in the river, but many will be running and resting. You'll catch more if you target those specific spots, like the tails of pools above long rapids, where running fish often gather to rest, rather than working down the whole length of long pools.

If you know that some hot spots work best at a certain water height, make sure you are there as the river drops. Small pods of running salmon usually reveal themselves as they make their way slowly upriver. Intercept them at their next likely lie. Even if you exhaust yourself running upstream, the result will be worth it!

WHAT TIME OF DAY IS BEST?

This is an impossible question. Fish that need to eat to survive have feeding habits that reflect the availability of their prey. There are no such markers for salmon. Changing weather and conditions are a big influence on the 'vulnerability' of salmon and are probably more important than the time of day.

For example, when spate rivers rise and become very dirty, your chance of success is low, but before long the river level peaks and begins to drop and clear. These conditions offer the best chance of all. It matters not one jot what time of day it is when these conditions arrive. These rivers fall rapidly, so 'perfect' conditions do not last long.

But what about the best time of day when conditions are pretty constant? Is there a time when your chances are better?

First light or dusk?

Surprisingly, many salmon fly fishers do not rate first light and the first few hours of daylight as a great time. If the weather is hot and bright, the early hours are certainly very much better than the middle of the day when the sun is blazing down, but the evening is a better bet.

Some salmon run at night. There are lots of examples of salmon leaving deep holding pools as night begins to fall and running into faster, shallower water where they are much more likely to take a fly.

Other 'taking' times

Salmon 'taking' times do occur. Unfortunately, they are entirely unpredictable. The fisher who is on the river longest is the most likely to find one!

Almost every salmon fisher can tell a tale of catching a fish at, say, 11 a.m. On returning to the fishing hut in triumph, they learn that their fellow fishers all caught one at exactly the same time, despite the fact that everyone had been flogging away since dawn.

So, a vital piece of advice is this. If you are lucky enough to land a salmon, do not waste a moment in weighing, photographing and admiring it. Your very best chance of catching another one is slipping away with every moment that you do not have a fly in the water. The 'taking' time may be fleeting. Do not waste it.

SUMMARY

Where and when:

◆ Do not fish in 'dead' water.

◆ 'Live' water has flow and depth that provides comfort and security.

◆ Features i.e. 'creases', 'gentler streams', 'ridges, rocks and outcrops' and 'pool tail upslopes' create the most favourable salmon 'lies'.

◆ Changes in water height have the biggest influence on where salmon rest and reside.

◆ The single-minded fly fisher plans to take advantage of conditions, good or bad.

◆ The fly fisher who keeps their fly in the water for longest discovers the 'taking' times.

◆ The very best time to hook a salmon is immediately after you caught the last one!

THIRTEEN
WADING: AN ESSENTIAL SKILL

A salmon fly fisher spends a lot of time in the water. Almost all salmon fly fishing is 'downstream-and-across'. Where you stand creates the pivot of the cast. It is the critical element in fly presentation. You may need to be a bold wader to get to the right spot.

If you are a timid wader, afraid of fast currents or a treacherous river bed, you may struggle to move quickly enough through a pool. Or you may avoid likely streams altogether.

In contrast, sometimes good fly presentation depends on not wading at all.

Some salmon fly fishers wade through likely lies in a pool and then complain that the fish they have spent an hour disturbing are not taking! Fishers who would instinctively 'stalk' a likely trout stream seem unable to stop themselves leaping into a salmon pool and charging across it until they get to their wader tops. The purpose of Chapters 12 to 15 is to help you develop this essential skill.

WHICH WADERS?

The choice of wader material . . . breathable, neoprene or PVC . . . is a matter of comfort and cost. What is much more important is the sole of the waders' boots. This can be a matter of life and death. Most wader manufacturers offer a choice of boot-footed or stocking-foot waders. If you choose the stocking-foot option you have the advantage of choosing separate boots that can give much more ankle support, which many welcome, and a wider range of sole materials.

You could even splash out on more than one pair of boots to provide alternative sole materials that are best suited to the range of river beds and wading challenges you may meet.

THERE IS NO 'RIGHT' CHOICE OF WADER SOLES

Before you select from the options available, it is wise to think about the waders themselves. It may sound obvious, but they should fit comfortably. Boot size can be difficult to get right when you have to get them round a neoprene foot and a thick pair of socks. Too tight is painful, but too big does not help you feel stable in a fast stream.

Do not buy waders or boots without trying them on with care. It is equally important to get the right leg length for chest or waist-high waders. If the legs are too long, they will ruffle around your knees and chafe against each other . . . and soon be leaking.

It is also wise to choose boots with wide soles. The more surface area there is in contact with the river bed, the better.

PVC WADERS

If you are in a job that demands deep wading, you can bet that your employer will buy chest-high waders made from good-quality PVC. Such waders are roomy, very tough, long-lasting and easy to repair. They do not keep out the cold and you'll sweat in them in warm weather. But they are cheap.

BREATHABLE WADERS

If you are a salmon fly fisher, you will inevitably buy chest-high waders made from a breathable material such as Gore-Tex. These waders will be tight-fitting, easily punctured, unlikely to last two seasons and are tricky to repair. They do not keep out the cold but are more comfortable in warm weather. Worst of all, they are very expensive and, if you are wading in cold water, you will need 'layers' of underclothes to keep warm.

If you complain to your supplier that, after a few months' use, your breathable waders are leaking, they will test them and find small pin pricks that the water seeps through. They will inform you, as if it is your fault, that you must have tramped through 'undergrowth'. What else do they think covers river banks!

NEOPRENE

There is a third choice. Waders made from 3.5mm neoprene are tight-fitting, cheap, tough, easy to repair and long-lasting. Their greatest benefit is that they keep you warm if you are spending the day up to your waist in freezing water. Their downside is that if you are only wading intermittently and it is a warm day, you will melt inside them. However, they are made for anglers and you can buy 'stocking feet' waders and use your wading boots with them.

SOLE MATERIAL

Studs

The choice of sole material is not easy, especially as soles made with deep-ribbed, 'improved' composite materials are constantly coming onto the market. Although most help to grip the river bed well, most experienced salmon anglers like to see them enhanced with metal studs. There is no doubt that metal studs do improve grip, and you can buy them separately and screw them into a boot's sole yourself. Studs are especially valuable where you are faced with smooth, rounded granite, the fabled 'greased cannon balls' found on some rivers in northern Scotland, or on rivers like Aberdeenshire's River Dee, which has many smooth, steep-sided rocks to navigate.

The downside of studs is that when grip is lost and you slip, they can be hard to dig in again. They do not aid recovery! Lots of people slip when negotiating dry stones, perhaps when getting out of the river or even on the path to get there.

Felt

This weakness encourages some to choose felt soles instead. There is no doubt that felt is the best material for the soles of waders where you spend a lot of time negotiating the wet surfaces of weed or algae-covered rocks, which can be lethally slippery when wearing any other sole. Felt is pretty secure on all rocky surfaces.

It has a downside too, usually when you get out of the river, because felt is positively dangerous on wet grass. Many fishers have been injured trying to clamber up a steep, grass-covered river bank which feels like ice underfoot when you are wearing felt soles.

Composite, studded and felt soles are all fine if you fish a 'comfortable' river with a mostly gravel bed. Felt wears out first.

So, there are no perfect soles for waders. Some experienced fly fishers believe in a compromise. Some bestselling modern boots have a deep-ribbed composite heel with a studded felt sole to provide the best of all worlds. Choose boots that are best suited to the river you fish.

HOW TO WADE SAFELY

The more you practise wading and the more you get to know the river bed you have to navigate, the more competent and confident you become. Confidence plays a large part in wading. If you believe you will manage to stay upright you probably will, and you learn to trust your ability to retain your balance. Everyone slips from time to time. What matters is your confidence in your power of recovery.

At first, take careful note of the surfaces and substratum you have to navigate. Experiment to 'feel' how they are best approached. Take your time. Try to keep as much of the sole of your boots in contact as possible. Slide the sole slowly across the bottom rather than taking steps. Do not move one foot until the other is securely grounded.

Fast-flowing water can sweep you off your feet. It is safer to work across a fast stream at an upstream angle than it is to walk downstream.

WADING STAFFS

Use a wading staff. A third leg is a wonderful aid to stability in the water and they are equally useful to help you get up a steep bank. A staff should be a comfortable length so that it easily comes to hand. It must be heavily weighted at the bottom end or it will be swept away when you need it most. Your staff should be permanently attached to you by a cord looped over one shoulder (see Figure 5).

Wading staffs have a downside too. When fishing down a pool with easy wading such as over firm gravel, and it is hanging unused in front of you, it can become more of a tripping hazard than an aid. Use common sense.

FALLING IN

If the worst happens, do not panic and do not try to swim. Your waders and clothes are full of air so if you just lie on your back, spread your arms and lift your feet, you will definitely 'float' downstream. The chances are you will soon be beached like a whale in shallow water where you can turn over and crawl out.

This emergency plan works much better, but your response should be just the same, if you are wearing an automatic life-jacket. Many angling suppliers now sell fly fishing waistcoats that incorporate a life-jacket. Buy one and get it tested regularly!

WHY DO FLY FISHERS WADE?

The first reason is more about casting than fishing. No one can cast, especially with a double-handed rod, unless the line is extended out in a straight line below the rod tip. You get into the water to ensure there is a flow beneath the rod tip to straighten the line. And, obviously, you may have to wade to get close enough to likely lies if you are fishing a wide river that demands long casting.

The second reason for wading is to get into the best position to present a fly.

Whether you are trying to get a heavy sinking line down towards the bottom in cold water, or to skate a tiny fly through a well-oxygenated stream in the summer, there will be one place to stand, in the water or out, that provides the best chance to ensure that, as the fly appears in the salmon's sight line, it is moving attractively.

'DOWNSTREAM-AND-ACROSS'

Mostly, you cast 'downstream-and-across' and the angle of the cast, the vagaries of the river's currents and whether or not you choose to retrieve line all influence how the fly on the end of the leader behaves. But what is critical is where you are standing because you are the pivot that dictates how the fly swings across the river.

There is one vital compromise to be made. It is no good wading out to the perfect spot for fly presentation if it means scaring every salmon in the pool by splashing through their lies. Salmon, even if they remain in their lies or seem tolerant of wading, have not lost their senses during their time at sea. They can hear you, see you and feel the vibrations you create when wading. Disturbing them may not chase them out of the pool, but you can bet it alarms a potentially 'vulnerable' fish, perhaps the only one of many that is not 'switched-off' and would have taken a fly.

MAKE A PLAN – WORK OUT YOUR PATHWAY

All this means that before you start wading down a salmon pool, you must have a plan. There will be a correct wading pathway that should be followed. It is definitely not just 'start at the top, and wade down to the tail' as so many Scottish ghillies advise. It will be a compromise. If you have not got an expert guide to help, it may take several walks down a pool to work out the best line. Only by fishing it can you be sure of the vagaries of the current and changing depth.

The following chapter uses a real example to help to read a pool at different water heights and seasons.

HOW QUICKLY SHOULD YOU WADE DOWN A POOL?

When you stand at the head of a salmon pool and have decided on the path you will wade down it, you have a final decision to make. How fast should you move through it? Do you want to cover thoroughly every centimetre of it with your fly, or are you going to race through? There are different views in the salmon fishing brotherhood.

The most experienced fly fishers tend to vote in favour of speed. There is logic behind this view.

A 'VULNERABLE' FISH

Salmon do not feed in fresh water and no one knows why any salmon ever takes a fly. Most salmon, most of the time, ignore the flies they see. But occasionally one becomes 'vulnerable' and will take a fly. We do not know how long this 'vulnerability' lasts.

So, as you stand at the top of your chosen salmon pool, you can only hope there is a 'vulnerable' fish there. If so, there is a good chance it will take any well-presented fly it sees. The imperative is to get a fly in front of it before its 'vulnerability' wears off. Get to it quickly! It will not need a second chance.

Equally, one may become 'vulnerable' at any time. You have a better chance of colliding with it if you fish through a pool quickly two or three times, rather than fishing it through very slowly and just once.

FIND A RHYTHM

Try to find a comfortable wading and casting rhythm. Even in those rivers where wading is difficult, a sensible approach is to cast, fish the cast round downstream and then retrieve the fly line to its optimum casting length at the same time as you take two or three good steps forward before making the next cast.

If the river bed is very uneven, you will not be able to move and to retrieve the line at the same time, as you need to use your wading staff to walk forward.

Simply retrieve the line first, remaining alert for a take, before moving forward.

Overall, the aim is not to make the same cast twice. Ensure they are close enough, i.e. about two metres apart, so that every salmon in the pool does see the fly.

SUMMARY

◆ Choose good-fitting waders/boots with soles suited to the river you are fishing.

◆ It takes practice to wade safely. Be bold. Confidence will come.

◆ Wear an automatic life-jacket.

◆ Wading is the key to good fly presentation.

◆ Plan a wading 'path' through each pool.

◆ Wade quickly!

FOURTEEN
CHOOSING A FLY LINE

Ninety per cent of all salmon fly fishing is with a floating line. The depth at which a fly at the end of the line should be fished depends mostly on temperature. Experience tells us that salmon take flies fished well up in the water when water temperatures have risen in summer and autumn. This is when most salmon fishing takes place.

An exception is some rivers in the British Isles which, unlike rivers further north in Europe or in Alaska, are almost never frozen over, and are blessed with an early run of 'spring' Atlantic Salmon. The fish run between January and April when the river temperatures are usually around five degrees centigrade. At these temperatures the salmon tend to hug the bottom and migrate slowly upstream. They are caught on deeply sunk flies using sinking fly lines.

HISTORY

A hundred years ago, all salmon fly fishers used silk lines which sank slowly as they absorbed water. If there was faster-flowing water in the middle of a stream, the line would be bowed downstream by the current and the fly would be speeded up as it was dragged from the far side of the stream. The fly did not sink far. The fishers knew that the only way to get their flies well down, where they would be most effective in cold weather, was to use very big, heavy flies. And they did, often fishing heavy flies on size 2/0 hooks.

In the 1930s, A.H.E. Wood 'greased' his silk line to make it float. He pointed out that a floating line that was bowed downstream by the current could be easily lifted off the water by a flick of his rod's tip to curl it upstream. By 'mending' the line in this way the fly's movement was arrested and it crossed the main current more sedately. He convinced a generation of salmon fly fishers that a controlled, more slowly moving fly caught more fish.

PLASTIC FLY LINES

The plastic lines everyone uses today were introduced in the 1970s. They were an instant hit. Floating lines did not need to be continually greased and could be easily 'mended' as Mr Wood advocated. And lines that floated were much easier to cast.

Although all sunk lines need to be retrieved, and lifted onto the surface, before they can be re-cast, the manufacturers of the new plastic lines realized there was a market for lines that sank quickly for cold water. Today, they produce many variations on this theme, from very slow-sinking 'intermediate' lines to very fast sinkers. This includes the popular 'Scandinavian-style' shooting head lines. They can be cast a long way and are easy to re-cast when all of the 'shooting line' has been retrieved at the end of each cast.

FLY PRESENTATION

Most salmon fly fishers use a floating line most of the time because they fish in summer and autumn when the river water is warm (around ten degrees centigrade or more) and their quarry is willing to take a fly fished close to the surface.

The 'standard' approach is to wade downstream between casts so that their fly 'fishes' downstream-and-across as the line is carried down by the river's current while they are the stationary 'pivot' of each cast.

This approach is repetitive, but it is satisfying to cover a pool effectively. You come to appreciate the twists and turns of the current as it meets rocks and other obstructions, and the subtlety of fly presentation.

It is not easy to describe good fly presentation, but most fly fishers instinctively recognize it when they are doing it! It ensures that a fly 'swims' into a salmon's sight like a living thing.

What does this mean when we break down the mechanics of a cast and look at what happens from the fish's angle?

When you cast your fly across a river, the current immediately starts to sweep the line downstream. You are stationary, and if you do nothing, the line will end up extended below you. The fly on the end of the leader will follow the line round and will trace any movement or curves in the line exactly. If the current were exactly the same pace right across the pool (and it rarely is!), the line and fly would follow a perfect arc from where you cast to directly down below you.

GIVING THE FLY 'LIFE'

You are more likely to have cast across a stream that is fast-flowing in the middle where the main stream rushes through and the water may be almost still on either side. It is also likely to be slowed and/or diverted by headlands reaching out from the bank, underwater ridges and obstructions, rocks and changing depth. In short, most pools have complex, changing currents that your fly has to navigate. Your aim is to give this fly 'life' during its passage through the pool. No one knows why a salmon takes a fly, but experience suggests it is much more likely to take one that is 'alive' and swimming across the pool like, say, a small fish. You do not want it to drift downstream like a dead leaf nor to race across the surface unnaturally and faster than any living thing can move.

There are some exceptions to this general rule, and these are dealt with in Chapter 17. For now, concentrate on how to give a fly 'life' during your standard, 'downstream-and-across' approach.

CONTROL

How can you control the moving fly? The critical factor is where you stand. Your position in the stream creates the pivot for the line and fly.

There are only three other things you can do to affect its movement.

Selecting the angle of the cast

The first is to carefully choose the angle you cast across the stream. If you cast directly across, or even upstream, the fly will start to sink and the fly line will drift some way downstream before it gets below you, when everything tightens up and the fly starts to be pulled across the stream. If there is a fast current in the middle of the stream, and the line has been bowed downstream, the fly will accelerate downstream as it follows the line. This is OK if it is the fly movement you want, but not if it moves too fast.

If you cast at an angle downstream, the line will tighten instantly as the current grabs it and the fly will begin to 'work' at once. It has 'life' because it appears to be 'swimming' upstream as it crosses the stream below the extended line. Its 'speed' will depend on the pace of the current. Is it too fast or too slow?

Mending the line

The second is to 'mend' the line. Flicking the rod tip upstream, once or twice if necessary, can lift a floating line off the surface and remove the downstream bow caused by the faster mid-stream current. This keeps the tip of the line, the leader and the fly in a straight line, and as it tightens in the current, the fly 'swims' across the stream more naturally.

Retrieving line

The third is to retrieve line as the cast fishes round. This option obviously speeds up the swimming fly. This may be an advantage when the current is slow across the whole stream, but the more usual, and more subtle, use of retrieving line is to give more life to the fly when it passes through a section of the stream where the current is lessened and the fly begins to move too slowly e.g. around a mid-stream rock.

THE 'TAKING STRIP'

The 'taking strip' in the stream of a salmon pool is where a salmon is most likely to take a fly. It is where perfect presentation is vital!

This concept reinforces the need to wade down a pool as quickly as possible. No one gets fly presentation right the first time they fish a pool. No matter how well you plan your wading path to get into the right position for each cast, nor how you manipulate the direction of cast or movement of the line, you will inevitably realize that a slightly different approach could give better presentation, especially as you fish your fly across that critical 'taking strip'.

Everyone fishes more effectively on their second walk down a pool.

SINKING POLY-LEADERS

If you fish with a full floating fly line and a small, lightweight fly, it will skate across the surface if you fish down a very fast stream.

Although there are important exceptions, discussed in Chapter 17, a skating fly is usually poor presentation and has to be avoided. The answer is to sink the tip of the fly line using a sinking poly-leader. You also have to remember to shorten your leader too, or else a small, semi-buoyant fly will still pop up to the surface.

Poly-leaders come in various lengths between one and four metres and they have different sink rates from 'intermediate' through to 'extra-fast sinking'. Their effect is probably less than you might imagine. In very fast water even a long, fast-sinking poly-leader will only get a light fly down a few centimetres, but in slower flowing water, where you might have to retrieve line to give life to a fly, it will get the fly down a bit further. And this is all that is needed!

Many fly fishers who fish on bigger rivers have a 'fast-sinking' three-metre poly-leader as a permanent fixture on the end of their floating fly line throughout most of the season. Connected to a two-metre-long nylon leader, this tip prevents a fly skating in all current speeds likely to be encountered. And it can be easily lifted to the surface so that it does not inhibit the next cast.

If you are fishing on small, perhaps drought-shrunken streams around rocks and other obstructions, a fast-sinking leader may lead to annoying hook-ups, and a slow-sinking or intermediate leader will be the better option.

Avoid 'extra fast-sinking poly-leaders'.
Think very carefully before using long 'extra-fast-sinking' poly-leaders. They do sink very quickly. They pull the floating line behind them down too, so the fly line cannot be 'mended' easily.

They are also exceptionally difficult to re-cast after the line has swept round in the current. No cast, whether overhead, roll or Spey, can commence until the fly line is on the surface. The combination of 'drowned' floating line and heavy, leaden tip is almost impossible to lift and roll cast onto the surface.

They also compromise good fly presentation. The combination of floating line and heavy tip creates a steep angle down into the water. Any retrieve lifts the fly away from the bottom instead of producing a fly 'swimming' at a constant depth.

USING SINKING FLY LINES
Sinking fly lines are only required if you are fishing in cold rivers where the water temperature is around five to eight degrees centigrade. Examples are the rivers in the British Isles that are fished early or late in the season because they have runs of early spring and late autumn fish. Or early or late in the much shorter seasons enjoyed by northern rivers in Europe, Russia or Alaska. They are cold just after the thaw that opens up many ice-bound rivers and again as winter descends.

HOW DEEP?

Early in the season, low temperatures reduce the fishes' level of activity and their desire to forge upstream. They find comfortable lies, always close to the bottom, in pools where they feel secure. They are reluctant to rise to flies near the surface or to leap from the water. So you need to get your fly down to their level within thirty or forty centimetres of the bottom. This is often not easy to achieve!

Fly lines are thick and, no matter how 'heavy', they are swept downstream quickly in fast currents and the fly does not get deep enough. Fortunately, in cold rivers salmon avoid the fastest streams. They usually lie in water where, with thoughtful casting, it is possible to get the line and the fly down to the right depth and into the sight line of the fairly moribund salmon.

There is a simple rule. If you keep snagging the bottom in the pool, you need a line that does not sink as fast; if you never catch the bottom you may need a faster-sinking line.

SINKING LINES OR HEAVY WEIGHT FLIES?

Years ago, when the fastest-sinking fly lines were not available, all sorts of heavily weighted flies were used in an effort to get them down deeper. In practice, most fly fishers did not persist with them because they were almost impossible, and dangerous, to cast. Their weight also rendered them lifeless in the water.

Today, most fishers using sinking lines prefer lighter flies, usually plastic or aluminium tube flies. They can be given some extra weight with brass or tungsten cone-heads (see Chapter 16).

Even if these flies are fished with the fastest-sinking modern lines, they do not get far down in the fastest steams. There are big, wide, fast-flowing rivers in Norway and Alaska where, early in the season, several grams of lead on heavy spinning tackle is the only tackle that will do.

Their fly fishing season comes later!

FLY PRESENTATION

Presentation of a deep-sunk fly using a sinking line is not just a matter of casting and getting it down deep. The real challenge is good presentation close to the bottom as it crosses the 'taking strip'.

Salmon rivers are rarely uniform streams that you can cast across and enjoy the line pivoting below you in a perfect arc through water of the same depth. You are much more likely to be faced with complex streams tumbling past rocks and outcrops and changes of depth as you wade down a pool.

A sunken line cannot be 'mended' so, once you have chosen the angle of your cast across the stream, you have little influence on the movement of the line and fly. It is at the mercy of the stream.

HANDLING AND RETRIEVING LINE

Imagine you are fishing a saucer-shaped pool which has a strong midstream current over a deeper channel. The fish lie in this channel.

Your best bet is to cast directly across the stream, perhaps even slightly upstream, so that the line sinks quickly as it moves freely downstream. If you lift the rod and retrieve a little line as it drifts over the shallow water beyond the main stream, you will prevent the fly snagging the bottom. As the line tightens and the tip of the line and the fly reach the main stream, you can lower the rod tip to help the fly get deeper down towards the lying fish. Then, after the line crosses the stream and hits the shallower water, you will have to retrieve quickly so that the fly does not snag on the nearside of the pool.

The point is that most sunk-line fishing demands active handling and retrieving of the line in an effort to get the line and fly to follow the contours of the river bed. This is not easy with a long, heavy double-handed fly rod and no 'free' hand.

AVOID SINKING SPEY LINES

Casting sunk lines with a long rod is also difficult. To Spey cast you need to lift the fly line onto the surface before it can be swept across your body. You cannot do this with a sunken Spey-type fly line which has a long 'head'. Even though the bulk of this head is towards the rear and it has a long tip to aid a roll cast, there will still be too much sunk line in the water.

To cast more easily, you need a sinking, weight forward line with a very short head. You can retrieve more line before re-casting and should be able to lift the short head to the surface and into the air no matter what sort of cast is required to get over the river again.

Use either a Skagit line/switch rod combination or a Scandinavian-style sinking shooting head line matched to a rod that suits the river.

SKAGIT LINES

Short-headed Skagit lines are usually floaters to which you attach a three- or four-metre fast-sinking poly-leader. You are able to Spey cast with this set-up if necessary, but both the distance and the depth you can fish at are limited. This is good kit for smaller streams or for any one who struggles to cast a long double-hander and heavy sunk line all day.

SCANDINAVIAN-STYLE SHOOTING HEAD LINES

If you are fishing a bigger river, a Scandinavian-style sinking shooting head will enable you to cast a lot further and get down deeper.

The shooting head should be short (eight to nine metres), so an overhead cast is still possible in quite a tight spot after all the backing line has been retrieved and only the head is beyond the rod tip.

Whether you choose a long double-handed or a stout single-handed rod is really down to personal choice. There is no doubt it is easier to retrieve line with your free hand when using a single-hander, but many European fly fishers believe that they are not really salmon fishing if they do not use a double-handed rod. They relish the line control the extra length gives them in an awkward pool. And, perhaps more importantly, they appreciate the help it gives when playing a big salmon.

This is why most early-season fly fishers chasing giant Atlantic Salmon on the rivers of Russia's Kola Peninsula choose sinking shooting head lines and fifteen-foot double-handed rods.

SUMMARY

◆ Floating fly lines, unlike sunken lines, are easy to cast and they can be 'mended' to aid the presentation of the fly.

◆ Sunken, Scandinavian-style shooting heads cast a long way and are easier to re-cast than standard weight forward lines.

◆ Sinking poly-leaders are universally used to stop small flies skating on the surface when using a floating line. Avoid the 'extra-fast-sinking' leaders. They can make Spey casting impossible.

◆ Four factors control fly presentation. The most critical is where you stand. The others are the angle you cast downstream, 'mending' the line if it is possible, and whether you retrieve line during the cast. Give the fly 'life'!

◆ Concentrate on getting fly presentation right as it crosses the 'taking strip'.

◆ Sinking lines are needed when the water temperature is low. Skagit and shooting head lines are easier to cast and usually give better fly presentation close to the river bed.

FIFTEEN

READING A POOL

This chapter describes an actual salmon pool on the Findhorn, a Scottish Highlands spate river, as an example of how to read a pool and plan your approach to it at different water heights.

WHERE WOULD I LIE IN THIS POOL?

Before you start fishing down any salmon pool or run, you must plan the path you intend to wade. You have two obvious objectives . . . to cover lying fish and to be in the best position to do so. Start by thinking like a salmon and asking, 'Where would I lie in this pool?'

If you were fishing for trout, or any other fish we chase with a fly, the answer would be different. The most important factor directing a trout's choice of station in a stream is food. A trout must eat to live. The fish chooses a lie where the current delivers a constant stream of prey species such as hatching insects. Obviously this advantageous position may change from day to day as the food supply or the river's level changes, but the bigger fish will always take up the best lies and bully their smaller brethren out of their way. They are selfishly territorial!

Other factors will play a part. A lie that is 'comfortable', which demands little energy to maintain station, and is safe because there is deep water or cover which provides an escape if danger threatens, would also be especially prized.

A SAFE, COMFORTABLE LIE

Salmon do not feed in fresh water so food supply is unimportant. They need a 'comfortable' lie. Salmon need to conserve energy to convert their considerable fat reserves into eggs or sperm. They do not mind being in a tight shoal and may benefit from being together.

Being safe is also critical. European salmon do not have to put up with Alaskan grizzly bears, but all salmon seek out pools that provide space and depth. So salmon often gather together in rivers because, unlike trout, they are not forced to spread out in the constant search for food.

Every river has well-recognized 'holding' pools or runs where salmon congregate. These are often very short stretches of water. A 'beat' on a river may be many kilometres long, but in only a few metres of it do salmon take up semi-permanent residence.

These short stretches are the only part of the river that is worth fishing!

'LIVE' AND 'DEAD' WATER

From a salmon fishing point of view, these are the 'live' stretches. The rest of the river is 'dead' and should be ignored.

This may sound obvious, but many fly fishers start at the head of a long, well-known pool and simply fish mindlessly from the neck to the tail, taking a step between each cast.

They do not catch as many salmon as a 'guy with a plan'.

QUILLACHAN POOL ON THE RIVER FINDHORN, SCOTLAND

The Quillachan Pool on the famous Cawdor Estate water on Scotland's River Findhorn is a productive pool on one of the most prolific stretches of this spate river. It exhibits several characteristics that are found in many salmon pools. In particular, as the water level rises after rain, it becomes a different pool. A new wading plan is essential.

LOW WATER

In low water, at the head of Quillachan Pool (see Figure 23), there are wide, shallow rapids over a gravel slope before the river meets a steep cliff.

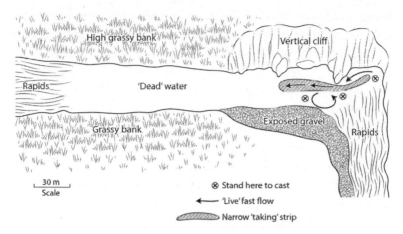

Fig. 23 – Quillachan Pool – Low water

The cliff forces the river to change direction by almost ninety degrees and this creates a deep, rapid stream against the cliff face with a 'crease' of slower water on its nearside. This twenty-metre narrow neck then hits a small outcrop from the cliff before the pool widens and falls into deeper water. The effect is a continuing stream down the centre of the pool but a turbulent back-eddy on the near side and still water near the far bank behind the outcrop.

Twenty metres on, the river's flow is concentrated in mid-stream and towards the far bank. Its flow is speeded up by the river bed getting shallower and by another small outcrop from the far bank which 'tightens' and concentrates the current for a few metres before it 'dies' as the pool widens and shallows.

From here the wide, shallow pool flows slowly until it reaches the next shallow rapids.

Little 'live' water
In these low water conditions, the only 'live' sections of this pool are the narrow stream and 'crease' at the neck and the short mid-stream flow

between and just beyond the two far bank outcrops. The rest of the pool, from the turbulent nearside back-eddy, along the nearside and the whole of the four-hundred-metre-long tail of the pool, is 'dead' water (see Figure 23).

Despite the very limited length of 'live' water, a surprising number of salmon take up residence in the deepest part of this pool when the water is low in summer and autumn. They reveal themselves by regularly leaping but mostly remain tightly shoaled close to the bottom in the deep water. Not all of them stay there.

From time to time, salmon are caught in the fast water at the neck of the pool. They do not shoal here. Perhaps individual fish 'visit' this fast water, which, not comfortable enough for a permanent lie, provides a few minutes' exercise in well-oxygenated water. These visitors are more 'vulnerable' to a well-presented fly than are their fellows in the deep water of the pool.

So, what's the wading plan in low water?

Fishing the neck of the pool

It is tempting to start at the very top of the pool and to work down the narrow neck, taking a step after each cast.

This is a mistake.

The better option is to stand still at the very top (see Figure 23) and to make a series of casts across the narrow neck, literally bouncing the fly off the cliff, but extending each cast so that the whole of the neck is covered. The aim is to swim a fly across the fastest water but then to 'hang' it and to retrieve it in the slower, flowing crease on the nearside of the main stream. This is where any visiting salmon will be holding station. Retrieving a fly steadily past its nose may produce the desired response.

Half a dozen casts, each one a metre or so longer than the last one, are all that is required to cover the whole section.

It is much easier to fish effectively here and to retrieve line using a single-handed rod, the appropriate 'weapon' for the Findhorn when the water is low.

Mid-stream

Once the neck of the pool has been fished, the next bit of 'live' water is the short mid-stream current below the first outcrop.

Again, it is tempting to fish this wading downstream with a step between casts, but this would not work. There is a deep back-eddy between the near bank and this short stream. You cannot fish across this 'dead' water because the strong, turbulent current both 'drowns' the floating fly line and instantly drags the fly out of the 'live' stream. Again, you have to stand still, just before you reach the turbulent section, and make successive casts, each one further than the last, that let you 'hang' the fly in the stream.

Finally, you get out of the water again and then wade in gently immediately below the back-eddy to enable you to fish your fly over the final stretch of 'live' water before the current dies below the second outcrop. You can walk down this final stretch if you wish, but standing still causes less disturbance. Again, make successively longer casts across the stream until all the 'live' water has been covered.

So, the most effective way to fish this low water pool is by making half a dozen casts from three spots where it is best to stand still.

Do not to cast over the turbulent, 'dead' water that creates the back-eddy which drowns the floating fly line and makes it impossible to re-cast.

In rivers everywhere you will see fishers who, having been told to wade down a pool from top to the tail, become frustrated and angry, by insisting on trying to work through a stretch of similar 'dead' water where no salmon will ever lie.

MEDIUM HEIGHT WATER

Like every River Findhorn pool, Quillachan is a better option when rain lifts the water level by thirty centimetres or so and pushes it up

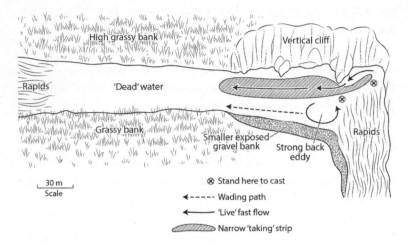

Fig. 24 – Quillachan Pool – Medium water height

the gravel on the nearside (see Figure 24). The extra water gives the pool vitality and extends the 'live' water where the salmon are likely to be found.

It does not make a huge difference to the first part of the wading path. Despite the extra water and the greatly increased speed of the current at the neck of the pool, salmon still make their way into this section and are even more likely to be 'resting' in the crease beside the fast water. 'Visiting' resident fish are likely to be joined by running fish, taking advantage of the increased flow to forge their way upstream, that rest here briefly before carrying on.

The correct approach is to stand still at the top and to fish a series of casts through the crease as before.

Moving downstream, the attack is the same. Stand still above the even more turbulent back-eddy and fish through the stronger midstream flow.

Below this, the final section of the pool is much more attractive. The flow is faster and the 'live' water extends right across the pool and much further downstream. This is the section of the pool where you are most likely to have success at this height of water.

The extra water 'pushes' the resident salmon downstream out of the deepest water and 'up' the gravel slope as the pool gets shallower. Perhaps it is the extra flow, or their lie in shallower water, that makes these fish 'vulnerable' to a well-presented fly.

HIGH WATER

After plenty of rain, when the river rises by another sixty centimetres or so, the character of Quillachan Pool, and its salmon, changes completely.

At this height (see Figure 25), all bare gravel is covered and the river is lapping over the bankside vegetation. The top of the pool where the river hits the cliff and bends sharply is a maelstrom of white water and foam where no salmon would be comfortable. Running fish will still be sneaking up on the nearside edge of this torrent, but here, and for about forty metres downstream, this is definitely 'dead' water and to be avoided.

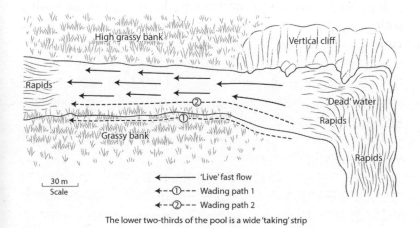

The lower two-thirds of the pool is a wide 'taking' strip

Fig. 25 – Quillachan Pool – High water

Below this, the river regains a slightly gentler pace that stretches across from bank to bank. Although there is a slightly stronger current down the far bank of the river marked by an obvious foam line, the whole river down to the rapids at the tail is 'live'.

Particularly 'vulnerable'

Every salmon in the pool has been swept out from the deep water and they spread themselves across the long, wide tail. And in clearing water with a strong flow they find comfortable, they are particularly 'vulnerable'. This is when, and where, a lot of salmon will be caught.

Fly presentation is easy. The current is evenly paced so a big, colourful tube fly, essential in the peaty water, that swings attractively across the current is all you need.

Two wading paths

It makes sense to have two wading paths down this long, wide stretch. The first should involve little more than getting your feet wet and casting about halfway across to cover the fish lying within reach of the nearside bank.

Then, second time down, wade out as far as the depth permits so that your casts reach across to the far bank. The two paths will allow you to cover every fish in the pool and any new arrivals running through. Then, after a short rest, and if you have still got enough energy, you can start all over again. There will still be willing fish out there!

A simple plan

If you are lucky enough to be fishing a wide, even-paced salmon pool that is well stocked with fish, plan wading paths that target the whole pool and work along them quickly and systematically. You are looking for the fish that are 'vulnerable'. You do yourself no favours by letting any fish see your fly twice.

SUMMARY

◆ Make a plan of your wading path before you start down a pool.

◆ Salmon seek 'comfort' and 'security' from their lies and are happy to shoal up together.

◆ Every salmon pool or run can be divided into 'dead' and 'live' water. Do not fish in 'dead' water.

◆ Salmon lies change, often hugely, in different heights of water.

◆ Do not ignore 'temporary' lies.

◆ Salmon pushed out of the deep lies by a flood become more 'vulnerable' to a well-presented fly.

SIXTEEN

CHOOSING A FLY AND GIVING IT LIFE

There are thousands of salmon flies. New patterns, with exaggerated promises of success, appear on the pages of fishing magazines each week. There is no such thing as an infallible salmon fly. Fly tiers keep trying. Salmon do not feed in fresh water. There cannot be a race to create an even better imitation of a favourite food. Trying a new colour, size or shape is pure guesswork. No one knows why a salmon rises to a fly.

If you are new to salmon fly fishing, start with fly patterns which have stood the test of time. These flies have caught thousands of salmon in different conditions and in rivers around the world.

This chapter describes a small number of these flies, their variations and how to fish them. You can fly fish for salmon confidently on any river in the world with this collection.

A SHORT LIST OF 'ESSENTIAL' FLIES
These flies have been chosen because they have caught thousands of salmon. They will catch thousands of salmon in the future.

The aim of this book is to convince you that a successful salmon fly fisher has to be able to cast well, no matter the weather or conditions, and should be a confident wader. If you use the best combination of rod and line and handle them cleverly, you will be able to present their fly to lying salmon even if they are hard to reach. Many salmon will ignore the fly, but if just one is 'vulnerable', it will certainly see and, hopefully, take the fly.

The pattern or size of fly chosen can be important, but having the 'technical' competence to present it well is even more important.

FLY SIZE

Everyone agrees that the colder the water, the bigger the fly should be. In cold water the fly should move slowly.

When the water reaches summer temperatures, the fly chosen should be small. And, often, a quickly moving fly is the key to success.

Most of the flies listed below can be dressed in different sizes.

A RED AND YELLOW TUBE FLY

After heavy rain, all salmon rivers colour up. Some become very muddy and take days to clear. Others, especially if there are big, clear lakes in their watercourse, will clear in a few hours when the rain stops and the tributary streams begin to fall back.

On many rivers, such as Scotland's River Tweed, fly fishing stops when the river is high and dirty, on the grounds that it is a waste of time. This is probably true, but only the salmon can dictate when the river has cleared enough to make fishing worthwhile.

The fly you need on the end of your line when the water is dirty has to be highly visible. A gold-bodied tube fly with bright yellow and crimson buck tail is bold and stands out even in muddy water. No matter the water temperature, it should be big. It should be dressed on a one and a quarter inch long plastic tube with a gold cone head, but the buck tail 'wings' should stretch back by at least another inch to create a fly that is nearly two and a half inches long.

This un-named fly has caught salmon in dirty water everywhere. Some fly tiers add an under-wing of white buck tail to a dirty water fly to seek even more visibility, but this is probably an unnecessary refinement.

Sinking line

The fly should be fished behind a sinking line or a floating line with a long, fast-sinking poly-leader.

When rivers are dirty and in flood, salmon abandon their normal lies and tend to tuck themselves in close to the bank where they find shelter along the 'creases' formed by grassy outcrops that would normally be high up the bank. Other fish may take the opportunity to run upstream, but they too will hug the banks and regularly seek shelter from the current.

The big yellow and red tube fly will continue to catch until the river clears.

Small version
Red and yellow are also two of the favourite colours found in salmon flies specifically used in autumn in the British Isles. For example, the Garry Dog, which was first devised in Perthshire, has been popular for generations. So a much smaller red and yellow, gold-bodied tube fly around three quarters of an inch long, or the same fly tied on a size 8 or 10 hook, can be used with confidence as the leaves start to turn.

WILLIE GUNN TUBE FLY
When the river clears after a flood, but is still high, a change of fly is called for. You will not go far wrong if you opt for a Willie Gunn tube.

Willie Gunn was a ghillie on the River Brora, over fifty years ago, when he invented the fly which still bears his name. The Brora was then one of Scotland's premier spring salmon rivers. Willie's fly is dark, like many flies that are attractive to early run salmon, but he wanted some highlights to make sure it was noticed. The black floss silk, or seal fur, body is ribbed with wide gold tinsel, and, before he tied in the black buck tail over-wing, Willie tied in sparser underwings, first of yellow buck tail and then orange. The original fly would have been tied on big single hooks up to size 2/0. Today, it is usually tied as a tube fly (see Figure 26).

A smaller fly
A Willie Gunn on a one and a quarter inches long tube that is at least two inches long overall is used in the cold early season months.

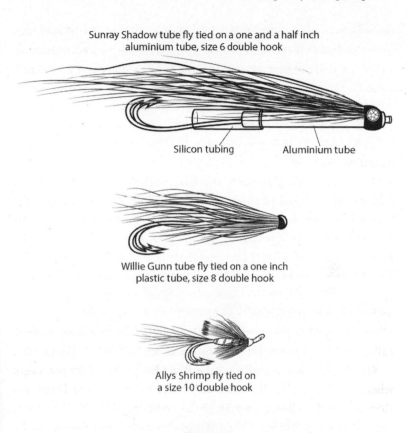

Sunray Shadow tube fly tied on a one and a half inch
aluminium tube, size 6 double hook

Silicon tubing   Aluminium tube

Willie Gunn tube fly tied on a one inch
plastic tube, size 8 double hook

Allys Shrimp fly tied on
a size 10 double hook

Stoat's Tail fly tied on
a size 14 hook

Fig. 26 – Variety of salmon flies illustrating range of sizes and styles

The same pattern is just as successful all summer long tied in progressively smaller sizes down to half-inch tubes or size 10 and 12 single and double hooks when the water is low and warm. In the smallest sizes the buck tail can be replaced by finer dyed squirrel tail of the same colours. This is another pattern that has been used successfully throughout the season wherever salmon swim.

In cold water, a Willie Gunn tube is the perfect fly to fish behind a sinking line and swung slowly to hang over deep-lying salmon. In warmer water, it does not need to be fished so deep nor so slowly.

What this fly should give you is the confidence to keep going. Confidence is the successful salmon fly fisher's secret weapon. If any fly is going to work, it is a Willie Gunn.

A SMALL BLACK FLY

At the other end of the scale from two-inch-plus bright and colourful tube flies is a small black fly tied on size 10 and 12 hooks. This is the fly of choice when the river is low, the water is clear and the summer has arrived.

Generations of salmon fly fishers have caught thousands of summer salmon on small black flies. The best-known pattern is the stoat's tail. The fly consists of a black floss or seal's fur body ribbed with silver wire, a sparse black hackle and a wispy wing of fur from the tip of a stoat's tail. If stoats' tails are in short supply, a black squirrel tail wing is just as good.

A small black fly is a summer fly. It is usually fished just under the surface behind a floating line or one tipped with a slow-sinking poly-leader. It can be used with confidence in fast water at the neck of a pool, swung across the slower, unruffled surface in the middle of the pool and, especially, towards the tail where the current will be speeding up.

As with all small flies, get it moving. Use the angle of the floating line across the main current or slowly retrieve it before it gets to the 'taking strip'. Then keep it moving after it leaves the 'strip' just before you re-cast. Summer salmon and grilse prefer a fly that is moving steadily (do not strip it too fast) across the stream. They can suddenly speed out of their lie to grab a fly that has already passed them. There are many variations on the small black fly (see Figure 26).

You can add Jungle Cock cheeks, but no one guarantees it helps. If there is a tinge of colour in the water, try one with a body of flat silver tinsel, a Silver Stoat. In autumn replace the black hackle with an orange one. This is a Stinchar Stoat.

Orange is a *de rigueur* colour for late-season flies, but it probably does not matter which variation you choose. You can fish them all with confidence.

ALLY'S SHRIMP

Over thirty years ago, Ally Gowans, a fly fishing coach from Pitlochry, a tourist town at the heart of Scotland, devised a fly which incorporated features from all his favourite salmon flies.

He wanted a shrimp fly, so, using red tying silk, he started with a tail of a dozen or so wavy, red buck tail hairs to make the fly at least twice as long as the hook. The back half of the body was red like a Curry's Shrimp. The front half was black like so many other flies. It was ribbed with silver wire. He added a grey squirrel wing similar to the successful Munro's Killer and tied in cheeks using small golden pheasant tippet feathers. These feathers also form part of the wing of many traditional salmon flies. He finished off the fly with a bright-orange hackle, another common salmon fly feature, and then coated the neat head with bright-red varnish (see Figure 26).

Ally tried out the fly on his local rivers, the Tay and the Tummel, with some success before offering it his friends and clients.

World famous

It took the salmon fishing world by storm and its fame spread far beyond Scotland. For years, nearly every salmon caught in Scotland was caught on an Ally's Shrimp. It was not surprising. Nearly every Scottish salmon fly fisher was using an Ally's Shrimp.

The fly was tied on size 4 and 6 hooks for use early season. In summer and autumn, smaller versions on size 10 hooks were just as successful. Then back to the bigger sizes as temperatures dropped and late autumn fishing got under way on the River Tweed in October and November.

Ally's Shrimp is a salmon fly for all seasons and one that has travelled exceptionally well. It is well used in Alaska, Iceland, Russia and Norway as well as in its native Scotland. It is not as popular as it used to be because other flies, like the Cascade, have become fashionable, but it has been, and is, so universally successful that it deserves a place on this list. Use it with confidence.

ORANGE SHRIMP

The Orange Shrimp is an Irish fly. Ireland's fly tiers are an industrious lot and there are many Irish shrimp fly variations. All these patterns have their advocates. They are designed with the canal-like stretches of some Irish rivers in mind. Here, flies are 'worked', i.e. retrieved steadily across the stream to give them life. Soft hen hackles help.

The Orange Shrimp was devised to suit the many Irish rivers, like others around the world, that always have peat-stained water.

The fly's tail is a long, bright-red feather from a golden pheasant's flank that is used in many shrimp flies. The rear of the body is medium or thick gold tinsel. A bright-orange body hackle is tied in and folded back over the tinsel. The front half of the body is black ribbed with more gold tinsel. The fly is finished with five or six turns of a long, soft badger hackle and a red varnish head.

This fly is one of the few Irish shrimp flies not adorned with Jungle Cock wings. It is normally tied on size 8 and 10 doubles. It is primarily a summer and autumn fly.

It is included in this short 'essentials' list because of its universal success in the peat-tinged water that many salmon rivers contain. It is also a bright 'you-cannot-miss-this' type of fly. It is always worth a run when nothing else seems to work!

TWO ICELANDIC FAVOURITES

Salmon fly fishers who visit Iceland are soon introduced to two unique salmon flies, the Red Francis and the Black Snaelda. They have been added to this 'essential' list because they are the most successful flies in Iceland. More importantly, they have also been successful wherever they have been tried across the salmon fishing world. Use them with confidence.

Icelanders claim both flies imitate shrimps or prawns, which swim tail first, so both flies have long 'feelers' tied in at the tail of the fly, and the rear of the body is built up to imitate the thorax of a crustacean, tapering to the eye of the hook to give them their unique profile.

Various sizes

Both flies are tied in a range of sizes and styles.

In cold water from snow melt, or early and late in the season, the flies are often tied on one-inch aluminium or copper tubes or Veniard's brass 'bottle' tubes to get them well down. In summer, they are better tied on size 8 or 10 doubles, fished higher in the water and moved smartly across the stream.

As with all successful flies, many variations have appeared as fly tiers and fly manufacturers have latched on to their success. The patterns given in Appendix Two are as good as any of them.

These two flies are now the most popular flies used on Scotland's River Tweed during the river's prolific autumn run. It's a long way from Iceland.

FLIES FROM ALASKA

All the essential flies listed above will catch Pacific Salmon in Western Canada, Alaska and the other north-western states of the USA, but very few American fly fishers use them. Very different families of salmon flies have developed here. Three successful examples are given below. Again, you can tie them on your leader, confident that thousands of Pacific Salmon of all species have succumbed to their charms.

Bigger single hooks

Most Pacific Salmon flies are tied on bigger hooks, usually sizes 2 to 4, than are used during the summer in Europe. This is because many Alaskan and other north-western rivers remain cold in summer since they are fed by melting snow fields. Usually, flies are dressed on single hooks reflecting the long-standing tradition of 'catch-and-release'. Although most salmon caught across Europe are now released too, the tradition of tying salmon flies on 'double' hooks and using 'doubles' with tube flies has persisted there. Whatever you choose, insist on modern, high-quality, chemically sharpened hooks.

Most of the thousands of patterns of Pacific Salmon flies are described by their originators as 'imitations' of leeches, shrimps, eggs or bait fish. A more honest description would be colourful!

Pacific salmon species prefer different colours

Alaskan fly fishers believe that Chum Salmon are particularly attracted to green and fluorescent green flies. For all Pacific species, red or pink can also be used with confidence. They believe that Sockeye salmon are partial to orange flies. Kings like fluorescent green too, but if the water is coloured many switch to black and purple flies. These colour choices are reflected in the flies listed below and detailed in Appendix Two.

The most obvious feature of these north-western flies is their bright, often fluorescent, colours and the use of modern, synthetic fly tying materials that are now being used with success by many European trout fishers. Are Europe's salmon fishers, who shy away from modern materials, being too conservative? These flies could be a revelation!

The Chartreuse Spider Web is certainly 'green' or at least 'chartreuse'. This colour has long been a favourite of American fly tiers in both salmon and salt water flies. This fly is prime choice for Chum Salmon.

The Purple Woolie Shrimp has a purple chenille body enhanced by a purple body hackle. A collar of purple marabou feather fibre adds a lot of life in the current. This is good for King salmon.

Sockeye salmon are attracted to orange flies and the Sockeye Orange has a reputation as an excellent Sockeye fly. It uses red squirrel tail for its wing.

SUNRAY SHADOW

Only a year or two ago, the Sunray Shadow fly would have been included in Chapter 17 as a 'minor tactic'. Today, using it has become a mainstream approach.

This 'new' fly was invented in Norway a few years ago. It is a new take on a traditional theme. The Sunray Shadow is a long, a very long (!), hair-wing fly (see Figure 26).

What is different is that this new fly is used in summer. Predecessors such as the Collie Dog were thought of as cold-water flies. A more startling change is using it as a fast-stripped 'lure' across the surface of pools instead of as a fly that was methodically used to search the depths of deeper pools.

The Sunray Shadow is a tube fly. Sizes vary, but most are tied on one and a quarter inch plastic tubes and the overall length of the finished fly is at least three inches, many are four inches long, sometimes a little more.

The original pattern was tied by Ray Brooks using black and white hair. It has been reported that the only hair he could find that was long enough came from the Cerebus monkey, but most Sunray Shadows you buy today will be tied using two-inch-long white buck tail under an over-wing of black arctic fox tail which is at least four inches long.

The fly itself is simple. You can use a bare white plastic tube or enhance it by covering it with a length of silver or mother-of-pearl mylar tubing. The under-wing on one side is the white buck tail. The wing on the other side of the tube is a similar-sized bunch of black arctic fox which stretches back at least four inches. Add an over-wing of two or three similar-length strands of peacock herl and the fly is finished.

Variations

Inevitably, variations have sprung up. Replace the white buck tail with yellow and you have a Dee Monkey.

Another is to replace both wings with synthetic material such as white and olive DNA fibres. The peacock herl remains a fixture. You can also add small plastic eyes.

How to fish a sunray shadow

This fly has proved so successful over recent years that it is now used wherever salmon swim. Some stories may be exaggerated but the fly is a great change option that often works when standard flies and tactics fail. The tactic that often works is to strip the fly across a pool behind a floating line so that it is close to the surface. A steady speed rather than high velocity seems to be the key. This may be easier to achieve using a single-handed rod. Another 'trick' is to cast upstream into fast water at the head of a pool where grilse or salmon are lying and to strip back as quickly as possible so that the fly follows a downstream curve in the current. Takes can be savage.

The other likely spot is across the tail of pools where fish lie where the current is speeding up. Again, a Sunray Shadow stripped across the lip of the fall where the pool ends can have dramatic results.

A first-choice fly

Some Scottish fly fishers have enjoyed so much success with the fly that it is now their first-choice fly at all times.

They use it early and late in the season when the water is cold behind a sinking line and fish it steadily and slowly over known lies. And they continue to use this big fly behind a conventional floating line and poly-leader combination when others are using much smaller flies.

They do use the fast-stripping tactic from time to time but report as much success using the standard down-and-across tactics they would use when fishing with a Stoat's Tail or Ally's Shrimp.

Whatever your approach, the Sunray Shadow deserves its place on an 'essential' list.

SUMMARY

- ◆ Today's strong, slim, chemically sharpened salmon fly hooks are a big improvement on traditional salmon 'irons'. Use them!
- ◆ Plastic tube flies with brass or tungsten 'cone' heads used with today's range of sinking lines are an effective combination.
- ◆ Good fly 'presentation' is more important than the pattern of the fly.
- ◆ The colder the water, the bigger the fly should be.
- ◆ Make flies 'swim' slowly and deliberately in cold water. Speed them up as the water warms.
- ◆ A shortlist of successful, 'essential' flies covers all conditions and should form the basis of all salmon fly collections.
- ◆ Two successful Icelandic fly patterns are now popular everywhere.
- ◆ Three Alaskan Pacific Salmon patterns demonstrate the unique, bright and colourful patterns used there.
- ◆ The Sunray Shadow is a recent addition to the 'essential' list. Try stripping it steadily just below the surface across lying salmon and be ready for a savage response.

SEVENTEEN
ALTERNATIVE TACTICS

Ninety-nine per cent of all salmon fly fishing is 'downstream-and-across'. The fly fisher casts across or downstream and skilfully manipulates the movement of the line to achieve perfect fly presentation as the current sweeps it across the stream. This is not the only way for the fly fisher to present a fly.

This chapter details some alternatives to the conventional approach. Some are 'local' initiatives. They are often tried as last-ditch attempts to save a blank day. Perhaps they demand more universal attention.

Salmon fly fishers are a pretty conservative bunch. This is not surprising. Salmon are a challenging quarry. Often conditions are against the fly fisher. Every salmon fly fisher in the British Isles has experienced low water conditions in the summer or autumn. British salmon rivers, unlike those in more northern climes, have no melting snowfields to keep water levels up if a stubborn Atlantic high-pressure system banishes the rain and raises the temperature. Salmon either stay in the river estuaries or retreat to the deepest, coolest pools where they do not respond to the usual tactics. It seems to make sense to throw in the towel and head home.

On the other hand, when conditions are perfect, you know that conventional tactics will work if you put in the effort. Salmon are hard won so it is a brave soul who departs from the tactics that do work to try something new and, perhaps, squander a fleeting chance of success.

This means 'alternative' or 'minor' tactics tend to be tried only during the worst possible conditions. Is that a fair experiment? Are you brave enough to challenge conventional wisdom? Some options follow.

SUNK LINE AND A BIG FLY IN LOW WATER

When river levels drop and temperatures rise, the conventional approach is to use smaller and smaller flies and to fish them behind a floating line. The places where good fly presentation is possible become fewer because the river's volume is less and its currents become slower. Streams over well-known salmon lies become sluggish, and while giving the small fly life by retrieving line is an option, there are more places where it does not work than there are where it does.

Sometimes the salmon abandon their usual lies in low water conditions. There is no point in fishing what is now 'dead' water. In low water conditions an alternative tactic to try is to head for a 'holding' pool where resident salmon are regularly leaping to display their presence. Do not worry if the pool is so deep and the water level is so low that the current through it is nearly non-existent.

Most Scottish and Irish salmon beats have such a pool. Put your double-handed rod away. Get out a beefy single-handed rod that happily casts a heavily dressed size 6 or 8 fly such as an Ally's Shrimp. Team up this rod with a fast-sinking line.

COVER THE POOL

The technique is simple. Start at the neck of the pool where water will still be flowing in. Cast as far downstream as you can and let the line sink. Work out how long it takes to get to the bottom. Retrieve steadily and smoothly. Your aim is to keep the fly as close to the bottom as possible. Work downstream. When you are mid-pool, cast straight across. When you get to the tail, cast upstream as far as you can. Cover every centimetre of the pool. This sounds easier than it actually is. You will snag the bottom. Some pools are littered with tree branches and other obstructions. If you persevere, you may be surprised by your success, especially if you concentrate your efforts early and late in the day.

This minor tactic may not work in all rivers at all times but it is successful enough to be always worth trying.

You may be worrying that if you pull a big fly across the bottom of a well-stocked pool you could be accused of 'snatching' i.e. trying to foul-hook a fish. Be reassured. This minor tactic has resulted in hundreds of fairly hooked fish in rivers large and small. Salmon seem to be adept at avoiding a fly they do not want to take. If you are still worried, make sure you use a single-hook fly rather than one dressed on a double or treble hook

USE A TINY FLY

As an alternative to a big fly in deep, still pools during low water conditions, do the exact opposite. Try using tiny flies. Nearly all salmon flies sold in fishing tackle stores are tied on size 6 and 8 hooks. In Alaska they are a lot bigger!

In shrunken rivers salmon usually retreat to deep pools. But some fish are always seen leaping or swirling, in shallower streams, such as the faster water that runs into the deep pools. Perhaps these salmon visit this fast water temporarily to get a quick hit of oxygenated water. At times, it seems these visits are more frequent earlier or late in the day. These fish are worth targeting.

Some fly fishers seem to believe salmon only take 'salmon' flies tied on big hooks. They are wrong. The best medicine for these difficult, 'stale' fish in pockets of fast water is a small fly, often the smaller the better. You will find it easier to present this fly in the narrow streams around rocks and other features using a light single-handed rod. They are more fun to play a salmon with on a shrunken river too.

To get hold of a small black Stoat's Tail dressed on a size 14 hook you may have to tie your own. Not many are sold in shops. It can be a worthwhile effort. Many experienced salmon fly fishers report success on tiny flies, i.e. size 14 where a size 10 failed. Try this minor tactic.

You will also catch small trout and salmon parr when using such a small fly, but treat them gently!

SKATING FLIES

Long before any one had ever thought of a Sunray Shadow, salmon fly fishers have known that their quarry can often be stirred into action by a fly that skates across the surface of a pool creating a visible wake. Sometimes this response is a swirl at the fly rather than a definite take, but that is encouraging. A fish that reacts this way may well take it properly when the next one skates over, or when one takes a different path.

There are several 'skating' fly techniques.

DIBBLING

On Scotland's River Shin and other north-eastern rivers nearby, 'dibbling' has been a successful alternative tactic for generations.

The tactic evolved on these rivers because they are rapid streams that fall steeply from the mountains over a large number of waterfalls, both large and small. The dramatic Falls of Shin are a big tourist draw in the area, especially when the river is in flood.

When the rivers are low, salmon residing or resting in the pools below the falls were observed 'visiting' the fast water. Anglers who fished their flies through this fast water were inevitably disappointed by the salmon's lack of interest. Then one bright spark experimented with the biggest, bushiest fly they could find (probably a large dry fly used for 'dapping' on nearby sea trout lochs) and they discovered this did, sometimes, get a reaction. The salmon swirled 'angrily' underneath it but, perhaps because it was dancing on top of the water, they failed to engulf it. The final piece of the jigsaw was to tie the big dry fly on a 'dropper' on the leader and then to tie on a small Stoat's Tail as the tail fly only 10cm behind it.

Literally dangling this end-tackle in the fast current using a long fifteen-foot rod now produced the hoped-for result. Salmon seemed to be 'angered' or attracted by the big dry fly but actually took the small Stoat's Tail fly anchored below it.

You may wonder if the salmon are hooked by accident when swirling at the big fly, but this does not seem to be the case at all. They are usually well hooked inside the mouth . . . and salmon are very careful about what goes in there!

This exciting minor tactic is not a panacea. It does not work all the time but it can work in any river with small falls and fast currents where salmon are seen.

'HITCHED' FLIES

On some Icelandic rivers the guides are obsessed with 'hitched' flies. This is a small fly fished behind a floating line that is so near the surface it creates a visible wake as it crosses a pool or stream. To achieve this effect, the guides half-hitch the leader around the neck of a fly or thread the leader through a hole made a short way down from the head of a fly tied on a small plastic tube. The effect is the same. The fly swims at an angle to the leader and is pulled up to the surface as it resists the current. These tricks are now redundant.

Several 'Tube Fly Systems' are now available from fishing tackle dealers that include 'Turbo Flow Cones'. These are small metal discs which can be fitted onto the head of a tube fly (see Figure 27). They provide the resistance required to lift the fly to the surface and produce an even more pronounced wake as they skate across the water.

Fig. 27 – Tube fly fitted with a 'turbo cone'

The dramatic, splashy swirl of a salmon taking a 'hitched' fly is part of the sales pitch ladled out to intending visitors to Iceland. And the guides are keen to deliver the goods.

That's fine, but it is a minor tactic and does not always work. Hitched flies are most successful when the water is crystal-clear, between ten and twelve degrees centigrade, and the salmon are fresh from the sea. Happily, these conditions are pretty common in Iceland!

WHY DOES IT WORK?

An interesting observation on the salmon's reaction to skating flies may tell us something about why they do take flies.

Salmon can sometimes be seen 'on station' in a stream in clear water from a vantage point above them. Suddenly the fish darts across to a particular spot, typically in the visibly quickening stream round a large boulder, and turns on the surface as if it is taking an unseen nymph or fly. Its behaviour is reminiscent of a feeding trout. The salmon always returns immediately to its 'station'.

Observers report that this behaviour is repeated from time to time but not at regular intervals. It looks like a response to a specific stimulus, such as something drifting through the 'target' spot, but nobody knows if this is the case.

More interesting from the fly fishers' point of view is the reported response of these salmon to a well-presented fly. What often happens is that a fly fished perfectly, which covers the salmon's lie and is clearly in its eye line, is ignored. But when the same fly swims beautifully through the fish's 'target' spot, it races across and grabs it.

No one knows why, but the lesson is clear. If you see a salmon rise, cover that exact spot with your fly. It may also explain what many Icelandic guides know, which is why there are some specific spots that can produce fish again and again when a 'hitched' fly crosses them.

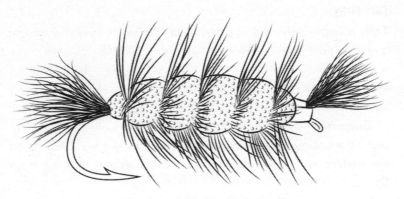

Fig. 28 – A floating Bomber fly

FLOATING FLIES

Not many salmon are caught on floating flies. They are nearly all caught on 'Bombers' (see Figure 28). A Bomber is a simple fly. It is made by tightly spinning deer body fur along a hook shank and then trimming it to a fat cigar shape. If you thread an orange hackle through this, you have an Orange Bomber. Green is a popular option. These flies float like corks.

If you fish this fly 'downstream-and-across', it skates across the surface and leaves a wake like a small ocean liner. This is a popular minor tactic used by those who are keen to claim they have caught a salmon on a floating fly. There are plenty of videos of this very dramatic event advertising salmon fishing on the salmon-filled rivers on Russia's Kola Peninsula. If you go there, do it too.

You do not need to go to Russia. If conditions are right, salmon will rise to a floating, skating fly on the surface just as confidently as they take a 'hitched' fly just below it. But they will probably need to be given more chances before they finally get hold of it.

Russia has an advantage; more salmon, so there will be some that are willing to play!

DRY FLIES

Only a few, very skilful and dedicated, fly fishers have ever caught a salmon on a 'dry' fly. Here, a distinction is being drawn between a floating fly skating across the surface, and a 'dry' fly (probably a Bomber) being cast upstream and drifted down over the head of a sighted salmon.

There can be no more heart-stopping moment than watching a 9-kg salmon lift its nose up to suck an Orange Bomber off the surface as if it were a River Test trout sipping down a mayfly.

Eastern Canada is dry fly central!

Such dry fly fishing meets with regular success in only one place. It is the 'minor tactic' that, year after year, draws salmon fishing fanatics to the beautiful rivers of Quebec, New Brunswick and Newfoundland in eastern Canada.

These rivers, such as the Grand Cascapadia and the Mirimachi, are not the fabled destinations they once were. Atlantic Salmon catches all along the Canadian eastern seaboard have declined, but the rivers have not changed. They still run as crystal-clear as England's world-famous Hampshire chalk streams.

In places it is easy to find salmon 'on station' over a metre down in water so clear that their every twitch can be seen. These fish can be approached stealthily from downstream so that they are unaware of the fisher's presence. Obviously you need to use a single-handed rod. It is no different from sneaking up on a trout in any clear water stream.

Water temperature

Water temperature is important. As with salmon everywhere, there is a fairly narrow band (around ten to twelve degrees centigrade) when salmon are most cooperative, and higher summer temperatures can put them off. Local experts advise that watching the response of a salmon you are covering is vitally important, but they do also target salmon they see 'heading-and-tailing' over their lie.

If the salmon does not 'spook' when you cast, you watch intently for its reaction to the fly being fished over its head. Sometimes they move towards it or they swirl at it without taking it. Give it a little rest before casting again. Persist if you do get such a positive reaction! Eventually the salmon may take the fly, gently sipping it down like a chalk stream trout.

Thousands upon thousands of hours are put into casting for salmon in Scotland and around the world each year. Very little of that time is devoted to dead-drift dry fly fishing. There are plenty of clear water streams where salmon can be seen, or they reveal their presence, so perhaps a trick is being missed.

NYMPH FISHING

There are many rivers in the British Isles, such as the Welsh Dee or the Teviot, which salmon anglers share with those who are chasing trout and grayling. Often, one of these anglers hooks a salmon on their trout tackle. Is it a fluke? Don't salmon have to be fished for with 'salmon tackle'? The answer is 'not always'.

The most 'vulnerable' salmon is the fresh fish that has taken up station in a shallow lie, perhaps close to the tail of a pool, where the current creates perfect presentation for the 'downstream-and-across' fly. Unfortunately, most salmon seek out deeper water. Here, the current often conspires to ensure most flies pass at least a metre or so above their head. A very 'vulnerable' salmon may come up to intercept the fly, but most do not.

GETTING DOWN DEEP

Grayling fishers in UK rivers face a similar problem. Their quarry often hugs the bottom of the stream. Recently, there has been an upsurge in a technique known as Czech nymphing. This involves 'lobbing' (they are too heavy to cast!) leaded nymphs upstream on a short line so that they sink rapidly to the bottom. They are trundled along for a few metres in the search for a hungry grayling. And they hook salmon simply because their flies get down to where a salmon is lying.

Salmon 'nymphing' is exactly the same technique. It can be used to fish blind in deep nearside streams where you know salmon are lying. It is an occasional tactic on rivers such as the Findhorn or on the North and South Esk in Scotland. It is almost the only way to fish a fly where these rivers pass through some deep, sheer-sided gorges.

DEEP-LYING, 'SIGHTED' SALMON

In the main, salmon 'nymphing' is a tactic used to fish for deep-lying, 'sighted' salmon in clear streams where the fisher's chance of success is much enhanced by being able to watch the fish's reaction to the fly.

For example, this tactic has met with considerable success on the short Bundorragha River on the famous Delphi fishery in Ireland.

The 'nymphs' used are either big versions of trout and grayling nymphs, such as Gold-Ribbed Hare's Ears or black and yellow Stonefly imitations, dressed on size 10 hooks, or heavy 'Bugs', dressed with orange or cream chenille bodies, similar to those used for sighted fishing for big rainbow trout in clear water ponds. All these flies need to be weighted, usually with gold tungsten beads, so that they sink quickly down to the salmon's level, which is often two or three metres down.

THE TECHNIQUE

The aim is to get the 'nymph' down as close as possible to the salmon's nose and to trundle it down past them in the current. You need to keep out of sight yourself. If possible, you pitch the fly in well in front of the fish so that it sees it coming towards it at its level rather than it descending onto its head from above.

Many fish will ignore the nymph no matter how many times you cast it towards them. Some salmon will spook, but they may return to their station within a couple of minutes and are worth another cast to see if you get a different response.

The reaction you want is the fish clearly 'stiffening', fins moving and becoming alert when it sees the nymph. This 'vulnerable' fish may let it drift pass several times before, if you are lucky, lunging forward to grab it or suddenly turning to chase after it when you think it has lost interest.

Very few salmon fly fishers have ever tried 'nymphing' for salmon. This is a 'minor tactic' that may deserve more attention if you fish on a clear water stream.

SUMMARY

◆ When salmon retreat to deep, sluggish pools in low water, try a big fly, fast-sinking line and a steady retrieve close to the bottom.

◆ If salmon are showing in fast streams when the river is low, fish for them with tiny flies.

◆ 'Hanging' a big, bushy attractor fly on a dropper in fast water with a small black fly 30 cm behind is 'dibbling'. Salmon take the small black fly.

◆ 'Riffled' flies are most popular in Iceland, but salmon in other countries take them too.

◆ Fishing dry flies upstream and drifting them down over sighted salmon is the ultimate thrill for many salmon fly fishers. Mostly it is practised in the clear rivers of eastern Canada. Perhaps it should be tried elsewhere.

◆ Nymph fishing for deep-lying, sighted salmon is just as exciting!

EIGHTEEN

STILL-WATER FLY FISHING

A Man may Fish *by T.C. Kingsmill Moore and* Salmon and Sea Trout in Wild Places *by Sidney Spencer are two of the most evocative books on salmon fly fishing. They describe fly fishing for salmon in the windswept loughs of Ireland.*

There are many lakes in the watercourses of salmon rivers around the world. Migrating salmon often find comfort and security in lakes as they wait until the time is right for them to run up the river's tributaries to spawn. Fishing for them is often by spinning or trolling or by casting flies at river mouths where shoals gather. In western Scotland and Ireland another approach has been practised for generations.

Traditional 'loch-style' fly fishing from a free-drifting boat is a magical marriage of wind, waves and watching for the strong swirl of a willing fish. Catching a salmon in this way, amid some of the world's finest scenery, should be on the 'bucket list' of every salmon fly fisher.

WHERE IS 'LOCH-STYLE' OR 'TRADITIONAL' FLY FISHING DONE?

In the ruggedly beautiful lands of the far west of Britain, high mountains and islands meet the Atlantic Ocean. Rivers pour down steep valleys to the sea. Often these streams fall into lakes in the valley bottoms before a short river delivers the water from these rain-sodden hills back to the sea.

Salmon that run such rivers do not have to travel far to reach the security of the lake. These lakes (known as lochs in Scotland and loughs in Ireland) come in many shapes and sizes. Some are deep, narrow and glacial in origin. Others are wide and shallow. They are all windswept, even in summer. They lie in the path of Atlantic depressions where they first meet the land.

Not all these lochs are salmon fishing destinations. Some may be too big or too deep, or not enough migrating salmon take up residence to make fishing worthwhile. Others offer a happy combination of depth, topography and bedrock that creates shorelines and shallows where waiting salmon become 'vulnerable' to a well-presented fly. The way to present that fly is from a free-drifting boat.

WESTERN SCOTLAND

The most famous salmon lochs in Scotland are in the Outer Hebrides. There are too many famous lochs and fisheries to list. To choose one, go to the Fishpal website. Click on salmon and then scroll down to Hebrides.

On mainland Scotland the most famous and productive salmon lochs are probably Loch Dionard in the far north-west and the giant Loch Lomond which is only 32 kilometres from Glasgow.

These Scottish lochs are mostly summer fisheries where grilse make up the bulk of the catch, although Loch Lomond also gets a fair run of spring fish from late March onwards.

IRELAND

Ireland is different. Some loughs there, such as Beltra, Currane and Carrowmore Lake (no one knows why it is not a 'lough'), are more famous as spring salmon fisheries. Fly fishers travel from all over Europe to try to catch their first salmon of the year there in March, April and May. It is a unique treat.

WHY DOES TRADITIONAL BOAT FISHING WORK?

Loch-style fly fishing is simple. You fish from a drifting boat that naturally turns broadside to the wind. You use a long, ten-foot or ten-foot six-inch single-handed fly rod with a soft, middle-to-tip action, a forgiving caster in the strong winds you will undoubtedly face.

The weather is critical. What the Irish call a 'soft' day is best. This is a day that is not too warm nor too cold, not too calm nor too stormy, and not too dry nor too wet. They enjoy a lot of 'soft' days in Ireland. These days create a 'good' wave, especially if the wind is not too gusty. Depending on the direction of the wind, the boat fisher can enjoy long drifts along a shallow shore or short drifts onto a lea shore.

The wind aids casting in front of the drifting boat. Everyone fishes with three flies on a three- or four-metre leader with two on short droppers. There are hundreds of Irish salmon lake fly patterns that have been used successfully for generations.

FLIES AND TECHNIQUE

Try the Connemara Black and Currie's Red Shrimp tied on size 6 and 8 hooks. A more modern 'wake fly' for the top dropper is a Muddler Minnow. You have to retrieve line a touch faster than the speed of the drift to keep in touch with your flies and to move them through the waves. You need to be constantly alert to the pull of a hooked fish or a swirl as it turns to take your fly as it breaks the surface. Your skill is tested by the way you work the top dropper fly through the wave tops and your ability to remain calm. You must wait for the line to tighten if you see a salmon's nose breaking surface before it sips down your fly.

That's it in a paragraph. Libraries of books have been written describing this delicious marriage of winds, waves and rising fish. There is endless debate on the design of boats, the length of rods, the changing light, the weather, the flies and the subtlety of touch that is 'loch-style' fly fishing. Read them all and join in.

THE JOY OF WORKING TOGETHER

Loch-style fishing is a two-person affair. The standard five- or six-metre traditional fishing boat was a wooden clinker boat that sat solidly in the water to manage the wind, not to be skimmed across the surface by it. Most boat-builders have now converted to glass-reinforced plastic (GRP), but the best are still designed with heavy keels to drift properly.

Normally two fly fishers share a boat and fish side by side, usually debating whether it is an advantage to be at the stern or the bow. If they are wise they will be accompanied by a ghillie, who will sit between them at the oars.

Two fishers work as a team. One can use a floating line, the other an intermediate or slow-sinker. They can experiment with different fly patterns and home in together on the one that is going to work best on the day. They can share each other's triumphs and frustrations. Other salmon fishing days do not allow for such companionship.

THE GHILLIE'S ROLE

As with all other salmon fishing, the secret is to be in the right place at the right time. If you are new to the water, this is the ghillie's role. A huge loch or lake is likely to be ninety per cent 'dead' water where no salmon has ever been caught. The potential productivity of the 'live' water is dependent on the wind. The good ghillie responds to the rise or fall of the wind, or sees its change in direction, and chooses a 'drift' accordingly.

In Scotland, ghillies have a reputation as taciturn men. In Ireland, that is almost never the case! Both will have years of experience to share. Help them to do so. Keen to try? Take a trip to Ireland to fish Carrowmore Lake.

CARROWMORE LAKE

Carrowmore Lake lies close to the small village of Bangor Erris in Ireland's County Mayo. If you keep travelling on the road through the village, you soon come to the larger town of Bellmullet and the Atlantic Ocean. The countryside is exactly as you expect in the far west of Ireland. It is peaty, windy and wet. The remoteness is romantic. The hills envelop you. Somehow it puts you at peace.

The lake is shallow and is coloured by the feeder streams that run off the surrounding hills and bogs. Very wet and windy weather can churn up sand from the lake bed and erode peat from some exposed banks and the lake becomes so dirty that fishing is impossible. Be warned, storms are common in western Ireland.

A narrow river, the Minhin, flows out of Carrowmore Lake and joins the Owenmore River on the other side of a few boggy fields.

THE RUN IS MONITORED

Inland Fisheries Ireland, the licensing authority, have a fish-counting station on the Minhin where it leaves the lake so their scientists know exactly how many salmon have run up it into Carrowmore. No one else does. Naturally, this does not stop the local anglers' rumour mill from churning out wildly different guesses!

Since 2011, the spring salmon run has been healthy and the authority has declared Carrowmore Lake as an 'open' fishery. This means any licensed angler can kill three spring salmon there, if they are lucky enough to catch them, from the opening of the season until 11 May. Although the season legally opens in January, few anglers venture out before the end of March. It is the reason why, when a visitor buys a twenty-one day licence, they are supplied with three blue tags. You have to carry these with you. A tag must be threaded through a salmon's gills the moment it is killed.

BANGOR ERRIS ANGLING CLUB AND SEAMUS HENRY

Carrowmore Lake is proudly, and efficiently, managed by the Bangor Erris Angling Club. They also have a long stretch of the Owenmore River which runs through the village. Their HQ, in more ways than one, is the West End Bar on Main Street, owned by Seamus Henry.

As they say in Ireland, Seamus is 'yer' man if you want to fish on Carrowmore. If you need a boat, want to hire a ghillie or just garner the latest news, then Seamus is who you talk to. His pub is where to do it.

Seamus is a 'quiet man' amid the chatter and merriment of an Irish tavern. He is proud of the atmosphere the club has created at the lake and of the efficient service he provides for visiting anglers from Ireland and beyond. With encouragement, he has much good advice for a first-timer. Anyone who has spent his life serving Mayo men with pints of Guinness and listening to their oft-repeated fishing tales has earned the right to be a little taciturn!

When you pay for your Angling Club day permit you are supplied with a brown tag. This is because the 'day limit' for spring salmon on Carrowmore is one fish. So, if you catch one and kill it, the fish has to have this second tag attached. You can carry on fishing but any others have to be released. In other words, the three spring fish permitted by your licence have to be caught on different days. Seamus likes you to return any unused brown tags so a deposit is charged as encouragement. This also means you return to the pub with the news of your success or failure. It keeps him fully up to date.

His records show that at least one spring salmon is caught from Carrowmore Lake every day in April and May when conditions let the boats get out. Some days it will be three or four fish shared between perhaps a dozen two-man boats.

Day tickets are available from 10 a.m. Most visitors and locals are off home or back in the pub by 6 p.m. But Carrowmore fish, like salmon everywhere, reward effort as much as technique. To do well, Seamus advises you to stay out until the light begins to fade.

UNIQUELY IRISH!

So there is probably nowhere else in Scotland or Ireland where you have a better chance of catching a still water springer from a drifting boat than Carrowmore Lake. But there is more to Ireland than fish. There is unique scenery, the 'craic' and laughter.

Two English visitors reported to Seamus that they had shared their boat with a ghillie who kept up a non-stop, optimistic commentary on their chances. He was also the only man they had ever met who managed to carry on rowing while he held phone conversations, firstly with his racing tipster, and then with his bookmaker on the merits of an accumulated bet. After he received a return call reporting on his losses, he delivered a complicated lecture to the fishers on the difference between an astute investor in the turf, like himself, and mug punters.

You do not get an education like that anywhere but in Ireland!

SUMMARY

◆ The origins of traditional 'loch-style' fly fishing from a drifting boat lie in western Ireland and Scotland.

◆ There are lots of good summer salmon lochs on Scotland's Outer Hebridean islands.

◆ Several Irish loughs and lakes offer loch-style fishing for spring salmon in March, April and May.

◆ Loch-style fishing is weather dependent. Pray for 'soft' cloudy days.

◆ Teamwork is the essence of loch-style fishing.

◆ Favourite traditional Irish flies are the Connemara Black and Currie's Red Shrimp. They work in Scotland too.

◆ Try Carrowmore Lake in Ireland's County Mayo in April. Fish on until the light fades.

NINETEEN

HOOKING, PLAYING AND LANDING

Experienced salmon fly fishers tell beginners the perfect moment is when their line pulls tight and they know, perhaps after days of trying, that a salmon has their fly in its jaws. This moment of connection is better than playing and landing their prize. Beginners disagree. A salmon is a hard-won fish and finally landing it is the triumph they crave.

Unfortunately, salmon have hard, smooth jaws with bone close to the surface. They also 'mouth' or 'nip' flies rather than engulfing them. Many salmon are poorly hooked and lost.

It does not help that there is conflicting advice on ensuring the best hook hold. Some advocate 'throwing' a loop of loose line at a taking fish. Others advise a strong, sweeping 'strike'. They are wrong. This chapter tells you what to do.

HOOKING A SALMON

If you are going to release the salmon you hook, you must be well prepared to handle it with care.

DE-BARBED OR BARBLESS HOOKS AND SOFT MESH NETS

The hook on any fly you use must be de-barbed or barbless. Removing any barbed hook from a salmon's mouth causes damage and extends the time taken to get it free. You can buy barbless hooks but every shop-bought fly will be tied on a barbed hook. The barb is easily removed just by squeezing it with a pair of sharp-nosed pliers. Using barbless hooks does not mean you lose more fish. It makes no difference at all whether hooks have barbs, but until anglers are convinced of this, hook manufacturers will continue to put barbs on nearly all their hooks and fly tiers will use them.

The other advantage of de-barbed flies is that they are wonderfully easy to remove from your woolly jumper or, perish the thought, any part of your anatomy!

Do not net a salmon that is to be returned in a coarse, knotted net. You will badly damage its sensitive skin. Use one of the soft mesh nets that are now readily available.

BEING PREPARED FOR THE 'TAKE'

Salmon fly fishing is a long game. You can fish for days before a salmon takes your fly. It is easy to be mechanically fishing downstream-and-across, admiring the beauty around or thinking about something else entirely, so there is sudden panic when a salmon takes. The fish is lost before it is hooked. Concentration is the key to success.

It helps always to watch the spot where the fly is in the water. You cannot usually see the fly unless it is 'skating' across the surface. But you know it is the leader's length past the end of the fly line. Thinking about the fly's location means you keep working on getting perfect presentation in the 'taking' strip and you re-cast quickly as the fly moves into 'dead' water. It also means you are alert to any salmon movement close to your fly if a fish shows interest. This could be an obvious swirl. It is just as likely to be an underwater flash of silver or the merest 'bulge' in the water's surface behind the fly as a fish rises to the surface to examine it. If you see anything, do not wade further. Make an identical cast. Cover the very same spot.

Alertness also helps you to remain cool and to react calmly when you get a firm take.

It also helps to hold the rod properly. When using a double-handed rod, the lower hand on the butt should be beside your hip on that side of your body. The upper hand, or the hand holding a single-hander, should ensure that the rod is horizontal, pointing down the line towards the fly i.e. the correct position for starting your next cast.

DO NOT STRIKE!

When fishing downstream-and-across, the current is so strong in some places that if your index finger does not hold the line it is actually pulled off the reel. Tighten the slipping-clutch on your reel to ensure this does not happen. You may have to adjust this clutch several times in the course of a day to cope with even stronger currents. Do not tighten the clutch further once the line is being held on the reel.

DO NOT TOUCH THE LINE

Your aim is to allow a salmon to take line off the reel with the minimum of resistance when it grabs your fly. And, of course, this means you must not be touching the fly line as the fly swims across the stream. Only when you start your next cast do you curl your index finger over the line to hold it tightly. Some beginners find this difficult. Their instincts are to grasp the line so that they are keyed up to act. Don't!

Salmon usually take a fly in a rather leisurely manner, rising deliberately before turning back to their lie. Acting too quickly pulls the fly from their mouth. Not holding the line and having to 'search' for it with your index finger and then clamping it tight against the cork handle after the reel starts to buzz as the line pulls out, gives time for the fish to turn and the hook to find a home.

The job is still not done. All fly rods flex and plastic fly lines stretch. If, when you clamp the line tight against the rod handle, you make the mistake of 'striking' by sweeping the rod upwards, you will undo all the good work. Striking bends the rod and hardly tightens the line. It does not help the hook to penetrate.

KEEP POINTING THE ROD AT THE FISH.

The right response is to keep the rod pointing at the fish to allow the line, which is now anchored by your index finger, and straight, to tighten. The tighter it gets, the more the hook point will penetrate.

Do not worry about a 'smash take'. You are using strong tackle. And hooked salmon rarely respond savagely. Their common response to being hooked is to stay in their lie and, perhaps, to shake their head. They rarely run until they realize they are in trouble.

So, wait. When the line is as tight as a drum, you can lift the rod and start to play the fish. It is the salmon's turn to panic now.

WHAT IF I AM RETRIEVING LINE?

Sometimes you will be retrieving line when a salmon takes the fly. A savage, hard take of the sort you can get from a trout is rare. Sometimes everything goes solid as if you have hooked a snag, but you realize instantly there is a live thing down there. Often, you actually feel the fish 'mouthing' the fly as if it were trying to feel what it is. The 'rule' is the same. 'Do not strike!'

KEEP RETRIEVING LINE

The right thing to do is to keep retrieving at the same speed as if you feel nothing. If it is a 'solid' take this will sink the hook and you will not be able to retrieve further. If the take is gentler, you may be surprised how much more line you may be able to pull back, still feeling the taking salmon, until it goes solid too. But it will and you will almost have guaranteed a strong hook hold.

EXCEPTIONS TO THE RULE

Loch-style fishing

One exception to the no-strike rule is when you are fly fishing from a drifting boat and, at the end of the retrieve, lift the rod to stroke the top dropper fly across the waves. This is a critical time. It is exactly the moment when a following fish may finally decide to take the fly as it starts to escape through the water surface. And, as you have started to lift the rod, there is not a straight line for the fish to tighten.

There are two things you must do.

Firstly, don't not react instinctively as you would to a rising trout, which can take and spit out a fly instantly. You must give the salmon a second or two to turn down with the fly in its mouth. Secondly, try not to raise your rod too high as you lift the fly to the surface or you will 'run out of arm' and will not be able to drive the hook into the fish by 'striking' firmly with the rod. Get into the habit of moving the top dropper over the surface with a sideways movement rather than an upward one.

Dry fly and nymph fishing

If you are lucky enough to be using a single-handed rod to fish a dead drifted dry fly over a salmon's head or trying to tempt a deep-lying one with a nymph, you will see the fish take the fly. Again, the take is likely to be deliberate. You have to remain cool and to react positively, not instantly. When you are sure the fly is in the fish's mouth, strike hard!

PLAYING A SALMON

Even a small salmon, such as a grilse or a silver, can be a handful to play in a fast-moving river. You only have to hook a dead weight such as a tree branch or plastic bag in a fast current to understand the added difficulty you face playing a strong, lively, big fish in the same current.

This is why it is important to ignore the oft-quoted advice to 'get downstream of a salmon you are playing'. Salmon are lost if a fisher, following this bad advice, keeps walking downstream and literally pulls a fish, which refuses to run upstream, into rapids or over the falls at the tail of a pool.

When this happens, you are in trouble. You probably have no choice but to follow it, because the fish, unbalanced by being hooked, cannot prevent itself being swept downstream. Angling literature is full of tall tales of hooked, giant salmon in rivers such as Norway's Alta and Canada's Grand Cascapadia being perilously pursued by brave fishers in flimsy boats through white-water rapids until their quarry could be landed in quieter waters below. If you have not got a boat, good luck!

HOLD YOUR GROUND

The sensible thing to do when you hook a salmon is to hold your ground until you both decide what to do. What is important is to prevent a fish getting into a very fast current, if possible. Some salmon set off on long runs when they realize they are in trouble, but most give more dogged, heavy resistance and do not run far. See what happens and then take control!

GET OUT OF THE WATER CAREFULLY

If you are wading, you need to get out of the water. Keeping the rod arched over and the line tight is more important than the time it takes to get to the bank. Try not to fall over.

FIND A LANDING SPOT

On the bank you need to find a place where your prize can be landed. This is easier if you are being aided by a guide or ghillie with a landing net who can reach the fish in an awkward place.

If you are alone, landing a salmon is trickier. If you can find one, pick a gently sloping shore away from the main current where a salmon can be beached. This may be the only way to get your fish ashore, because if you are using a long double-handed rod it is practically impossible to get a salmon into the short-handled landing net many salmon fly fishers have strapped to their backs.

PLAY IT FIRMLY

It is important that a salmon is not fought to exhaustion if it is to be returned. fewer fish are 'lost' if they are played 'firmly' to land them as quickly as possible.

The basic, good advice when playing a fish is to keep the rod tip up.

It can then bend further to cushion sudden runs and dives while still keeping plenty of pressure on the hooked fish. If your rod is not well bent, you are being too gentle. Rods will always bend further!

If the fish really does set off for the horizon, you have to let it take line as it pulls the rod tip down. No matter how strong your arm, you cannot resist the power of a strong salmon to pull the rod down to the horizontal if you do not concede line. If you do not give line, the leader or tippet may break, the hook may straighten or, most likely, the hook will rip out! So, give line reluctantly and make your salmon fight for every centimetre. As soon as it stops running, retrieve line and put it under pressure again. Keep it under control.

All salmon panic anew, and will make a final run, when they are pulled into shallow water. Be prepared for this, but be firm with the fish to stop it getting too far.

THE FIGHT IS OVER

As the fight comes to a close you can draw it over a landing net or, if you get it into very shallow water, a salmon will fall onto its side because it cannot remain upright. If you keep cool and keep the line tight, so that it cannot get back into deeper water, the fight is over.

You have two choices. If you are going to release the fish, resist the temptation to lift it clear of the water. Simply get on your knees and sit astride it with your back to the river to prevent it sliding backwards. Remove the hook, stand up and help it back into the river unharmed.

If you want a picture, hold the wrist of its tail to detain it, but avoid lifting it clear of the water as, no matter how well you support it, damage is often done.

KILLING A SALMON

If you are going to kill the salmon, the way to get it out of the water once it is on its side is to get behind it, grasp the wrist of its tail tightly and then 'slide' it head first up the gravel onto the bank where you can deliver 'the last rites' with a 'priest'. This weapon can be bought from any good fishing tackle store.

Many salmon are lost at the last minute when an over-eager fisher attempts to lift a salmon out of the water after grasping the wrist of its tail but then loses their grip. The fish crashes back in the water, the hook falls out and it is gone. It is heart-breaking. 'Slide' it up the bank instead.

How to play a salmon is easy to describe. In the excitement of the moment it is easy to forget the best advice. Plenty of practice helps.

SUMMARY

◆ Use barless hooks.

◆ Use a soft mesh net without knots if you plan to release a salmon.

◆ Concentrate on keeping the line tight and the rod pointing down the line as you wait for a 'take'. Do not touch the line!

◆ When a salmon takes and pulls line off the reel, grasp the line with your finger and clamp it tight. Do not strike! Let the fish pull the line tight to sink the hook. Now you can lift the rod.

◆ If you are retrieving line when a salmon takes your fly, keep retrieving until it all goes 'solid'.

◆ When playing a salmon, do everything you can to stop it getting into rapids or other very fast currents.

◆ Play a salmon firmly!

◆ If returning a salmon, avoid lifting it out of the water.

TWENTY
PREPARING AND COOKING SALMON

Most rod-caught salmon are returned to the river so that they can make babies. But wild salmon is one of the world's great culinary joys. So if you are allowed to kill a fish from a sustainable population, you must give it the respect it deserves to allow it to grace your table.

Here's how.

THE BEST MEAL OF YOUR LIFE?
The privilege of fishing for salmon inside the Arctic Circle often has a bonus. A salmon you have just killed is cut into thick steaks by your guide. He cooks it over a birchwood campfire until the iron griddle sears black lines across its pink flesh. He may even anoint it with some dill-flavoured butter before he presents it to you for lunch.

A bottle of Sauvignon, chilled in the river's edge, will add a perfect touch of civilization to this wilderness feast. It is probably the best meal of your life.

KEEPING SALMON FRESH
Not everyone travels to the Arctic, but if you catch a salmon to eat closer to home, it is a sin to let the freshest of food spoil through bad handling.

On commercial fishing boats their catch is gutted as soon as they get it on board and before it is refrigerated. They know that fish rot from the inside outwards and that this process of decomposition is very rapid.

If you are keeping your salmon, you should really gut it as soon as you have landed it and killed it, even if it is soon to be frozen.

STORE IT IN A BASS

Any salmon left exposed to the atmosphere, even when it is not sunny, will dry out and begin to decompose. If it is a warm, sunny day this happens so rapidly a fish will be spoiled in an hour. A dead salmon should be stored in a damp, porous bag kept in the shade. A bag specially designed for protecting newly caught salmon is known as a 'bass' and can be bought in any fishing tackle shop or from any website. A few years ago every bass was made of natural, woven straw, but today synthetics dominate.

Under no circumstances store a salmon in a polythene sack unless it is in a refrigerator or freezer! Polythene is not porous, and even when the temperature is low, a salmon inside one will, literally, begin to cook.

Some anglers leave their salmon in a bass submerged in the shallows while they fish on. This is fine if the water temperature is colder than the air, but if they are similar, as they usually are in summer, it is better to keep the bass damp by regular dipping and leaving it under the shade of a bush. The salmon will be kept cooler by the water evaporating from the damp bass. Beware of wildlife that enjoy fresh salmon as much as you do.

If you can bear to carry a cool-bag and ice-cold blocks with you, so much the better!

GUTTING A SALMON: PREPARING SALMON FOR THE TABLE IS A SKILL ALL FISHERS NEED TO MASTER

A SHARP KNIFE

The first essential is a razor-sharp knife. 'Filleting' knives with long narrow blades are sold in most fishing tackle shops and are a worthwhile investment. You also need to know how, and have the means, to keep them sharp.

The best surface on which to gut and fillet a fish at home is a wood block or other surface which is sandpaper rough and provides some grip. A normal kitchen worktop or smooth, shiny chopping board is positively dangerous. Newspaper does at a pinch.

Before you start, you need to decide whether you are going to leave the head on a gutted fish or not. Many cooks like to serve up a whole fish, perhaps poached in a 'fish kettle' for a banquet or special meal, so it may be best to leave the head and tail attached. They can always be removed later. However, if you do remove the head and tail it makes gutting easier.

First open the fish's belly by cutting through into the body cavity from between the gills and then between the pelvic fins right along towards its vent. Do not cut into its vent: this will puncture its intestine. Instead, continue to cut through the body wall to the side of the vent and just beyond it. Try to cut just through the body wall so that the tip of the knife's blade does as little damage as possible to any internal organs. It is especially important to avoid the liver and gall bladder, which are not far behind the gills. The gall bladder will stain the flesh yellow if it is punctured. Be prepared for some resistance as you cut between the pelvic fins. Do not worry if you do not get all this quite right first time!

REMOVING THE HEAD

If you are going to remove the head and tail, turn the fish on the cutting board so that from a start point just behind the head you can cut down at an angle so that you just go through the backbone. Then carefully cut round the body on each side of the fish so that your blade hardly goes into the body cavity until you reach the long, ventral cut you have already made along the belly. These cuts should go in front of the pectoral fins on each side so that they remain. The severed head should now be attached to the guts, but not to the body of the salmon. Grasp the head firmly and pull it along, below the body, so that all the guts follow through the open belly. They will all come in one piece.

Only the end of the large intestine will remain attached to the vent. You can either pull this to free it or neatly cut the vent out. Now cut off the tail if you wish to remove it at this stage.

Finally, wash out the body cavity under a cold tap and you will see that all that remains is a wide line of 'blood' hard against the backbone which runs the length of the salmon. This is actually its kidney. It would not do any harm to leave it there and would not spoil a cooked fish, but most people remove it. All you need to do is to grasp the fish towards its tail with your left hand (if you are right-handed) and with your thumb inside its body cavity to give a firm hold. Then place your other thumb, facing towards its head end, at the rear of the kidney. Firmly scrape your thumb along the backbone to the head end of the decapitated fish to remove it. It is a messy business, but plenty of running water helps.

RETAINING THE HEAD

If you want to retain the head and tail on a gutted salmon, the method is slightly different. Cut open the belly of the salmon as before from below the gills to beside the vent. Now the tricky bit! Get your fingers round the guts to pull them out slightly so that you can get the point of your sharp knife into the body cavity up just behind its throat in order to make two forward cuts from each side to sever the gullet beside the gills. You can then pull all the guts out of the belly. They may not come out as cleanly as with the head attached, and you might have to separately remove the transparent swim bladder and the heart from between the gills. You will also have to remove the kidney with your thumb as before. This is a little more difficult as the blood and tissue remain the body cavity as you scrape it out along the backbone. Lots of running water will soon clear it away.

To do a perfect job you should also use a pair of very sharp scissors or some snips to cut out each pair of gills. Just cut through them top and bottom and remove them.

FREEZING

Salmon freeze very well. The best way to pack them is inside 30-cm wide polythene tubing. This is available from most fishing tackle shops and websites. Pat the fish dry using kitchen paper. Cut a suitable length (i.e. 50 cm longer than the fish) of the polythene tubing and tie a knot in one end, put in the gutted salmon, expel any air and tie a knot in the other end. Job done!

COOKING SALMON

SMOKED SALMON

Smoked salmon is a luxury food. In most salmon-rich areas you will find small artisan 'smoke houses' that specialize in smoking fish. They will be passionate about the taste and quality of their products. If you ask them to smoke a fresh salmon (not a poorly conditioned, 'stale' fish that has spent months in the river!), they will be delighted. It may make a change from the flaccid, farmed salmon they normally smoke.

The smoke house will be happy to fillet your salmon. They will be pleased you gutted it. There is no problem smoking a salmon that has been frozen, but the best comes from fresh fish used within hours of capture. 'Sides' of salmon for smoking first have to be marinated in brine for twelve to twenty-four hours before being cold smoked (i.e. it does not get hot enough to 'cook' them) in smoke houses where the floor is covered with smouldering oak chips. Secret recipes often add a unique touch of flavour to the brine marinade.

Your reward is two vacuum-packed 'sides' of salmon. You may prefer to ask for much smaller packets of ready-sliced smoked salmon. These can be frozen and will keep family and friends supplied for months.

RECIPES

Smoked salmon is used in many recipes. It takes a lot to beat a 'starter' of smoked salmon, lightly garnished with lemon juice and dill, served with thinly sliced wholemeal bread. Spread the bread with a light and delicate cream cheese, if you wish.

SMOKING YOUR OWN

You may be more adventurous and decide to smoke your own salmon. The equipment to do this, including oak chippings, is easily available. Most 'home smoking' is a hot smoking process. The fish, cut into small fillets to fit into the smoking compartment, is cooked and flavoured by the smoke.

FILLETING A SALMON

A gutted salmon that weighs around 4 kg can be quickly cut into steaks about 4 cm thick. They are a perfect size to be grilled or fried and provide an individual portion. However, if your fish is bigger or smaller, to prepare it for smoking or for any of the vast number of other salmon dishes, the fish has to be filleted. Filleting fish takes a little practice. Do not expect to get it absolutely right first time.

SHARP KNIFE

Again, the value of good lighting, a razor-sharp knife and a suitable, rough work surface cannot be overstated. If you are nervous of knife work, you can buy protective chainmail gloves to protect your hands.

Start from the tail end of a gutted salmon with the head and tail removed. If you are right-handed its tail should be pointing to your right and its back should be facing you. Cut carefully, holding the knife blade horizontally, so that you begin to remove the tail end of the fillet from the backbone. Cut so that you can feel the knife just touching the backbone and so that the flat blade also cuts through the skin just above the mid-line of its back and belly and leaves the adipose, anal and dorsal fins on the fish. You can lift the fillet from the tail end with your finger and thumb to check your line is right, but as you continue to cut you will also need to maintain some pressure on the fish with the heel of your left hand to keep it still. Keep other fingers high so that nothing is in the path of the blade. From about halfway along the fish, right up until the final cut, you will feel the blade cutting through the ribs where they join the backbone. A sharp knife will cut through them easily (see Figure 29).

When you have cut one fillet from the salmon, turn it over and repeat the process to remove the other fillet from the other side of the fish. For some reason this always seems the more difficult side, presumably because it is harder to get a good straight cut along the now more flexible backbone. It becomes easier with practice!

Discard the backbone and its attached remains.

REMOVE THE RIBS AND PIN BONES.

All that has to be done now is to clean up the two fillets.

First, you have to remove the ribs. With practice you will be able to get the rib cage off in one piece. Place the fillet skin-side down and hold it still with the free hand. The trick is to ease the sharp knife under the top of the ribs where they have been severed and then to run the blade, turned slightly upwards, below them. The whole rib cage, joined by a film of connective tissue, is all that should be removed.

Second, trim the edges of the fillet, including cutting off the pelvic fins and their supporting skeleton.

The most awkward job is your last task. All trout and salmon species have a line of small 'pin' bones embedded in their flesh in a line along the fillet about halfway between the line of the backbone and the top of the fish. If you find this line and run your finger along it, you will feel the end of each exposed bone. They start at the head end of the fillet and peter out about halfway along it.

They have to be removed individually! If you have strong fingernails

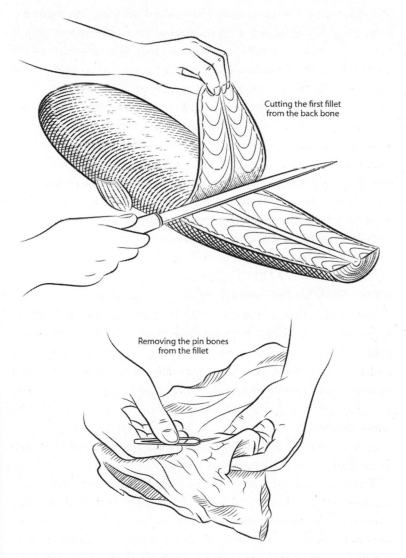

Cutting the first fillet
from the back bone

Removing the pin bones
from the fillet

Fig. 29 – Filleting a salmon and removing pin bones

you can pull each one out in turn, feeling for each new one with your fingertip as you go. They are much easier to remove using a pair of tweezers. You will find you tend to pull some flesh out with each pin bone, but this is minimized if you pull in the right direction to separate them from their attached muscle. If you want to be really clever you can run a sharp knife tip along the line of the bones to free them first. This task is a bit of a pain but some cooks prefer to do it this way (see Figure 29).

If the whole fillet or 'side' of salmon is going to be smoked and is marinated in brine as the first step in this process, you should delay removing the pin bones until the fish is removed from the brine. The purpose of the marinade is to remove water from the flesh, which 'shrinks'. The roots of the pin bones will now stand proud as a result and are so much easier to get hold of and remove.

ONE RECIPE: GRAVADLAX

This unusual method of preparation originates in Scandinavia where they know a lot about fish. It is a dish of raw salmon, cured in salt, sugar and dill.

Gravadlax is usually served as an appetizer, sliced thinly, and accompanied by a mustard sauce.

Ingredients
2 salmon fillets, each about 1 kg. It is best if they are identical pieces cut from the two sides of a filleted fish.

100 g sea salt

150 g golden caster sugar

8 black peppercorns, crushed

60 ml Absolut vodka

150 g bunch fresh dill, chopped, plus an extra 100 g

Method

1. Pat the salmon dry with paper towel and check all pin bones have been removed.
2. Place a double layer of clingfilm on a work surface and put one of the fillets on top, skin side down.
3. Make the cure by blitzing the salt, sugar, peppercorns, dill and vodka in a food processor to make a bright-green, wet mixture. Spread this evenly over the fillet. It is important that all the flesh is covered. Top with the other fillet, flesh side down, to form a sandwich.
4. Wrap tightly in the cling film and place in a shallow baking dish that holds the parcel snugly. Weigh down with a couple of tins or bottles and place in the fridge for at least forty-eight hours or up to four days, turning the fish over every twelve hours or so. Drain off any liquid that collects in the dish.
5. Unwrap the salmon, rinse off the cure with cold water and pat dry with kitchen paper. Finely chop the extra dill, and spread evenly over the flesh of both fillets.

The gravadlax can now be sliced (not too thin) and eaten. It will keep in the fridge for up to a week if wrapped in fresh clingfilm. The gravadlax can be frozen for up to three months. Wrap it in fresh cling-film, then foil.

6. When needed, unwrap, separate and slice. Serve on rye bread with dill and mustard sauce.

DILL AND MUSTARD SAUCE

Ingredients
Small bunch dill (about 20 g) roughly chopped
4 tbsp each Dijon mustard, cider vinegar, honey and sunflower oil
2 tbsp muscovado sugar

Method

Tip all the ingredients in a blender. Blitz until the dressing thickens.

SUMMARY

◆ Gut a salmon soon after capture.
◆ Store a newly caught fish in a bass.
◆ Use a sharp knife for gutting and filleting.
◆ Smoked wild salmon and gravadlax are culinary delights!

TWENTY-ONE
NEW HORIZONS

Catching a big salmon on a fly is the stuff of dreams for many anglers. Perhaps nothing can top that! But there are always other fish to catch . . .

Few anglers start out fly fishing. Most begin using a lure or a baited hook. It is easier. Catching a fish is success. As skills and knowledge develop, and fly fishing, probably for trout, is a natural progression. The technique, done well, is elegant. The trout is a worthy quarry. A successful trout fly fisher needs to be observant. The trout's eating habits, which are catholic and season dependent, demand careful study. Happily, there are plenty of trout. They are found in just about every country in Europe and most states of the USA.

Salmon are different. They are scarcely distributed, found only in cold, northern climes and have a short season. This relative rarity enhances the romance of hunting a big and beautiful migratory fish.

Salmon are a next step for the ambitious trout fly fisher. Unless you are very privileged, salmon fishing is a hard slog. You probably have to travel a long way to find them. The weather may be very cold and wet. Salmon do not feed and can be frustratingly disinterested in your flies. You will make thousands of casts between 'takes', no matter how competently you wield a fly rod.

Your reward is the world's most sought-after fish.

THERE IS AN ALTERNATIVE

Some fly fishers progress to salt-water fly fishing in the tropics. Here, the iconic fly fisher's quarry is the bonefish. This streamlined, silver fish haunts shallow coral atolls, lagoons and white sand-covered flats around the world.

Here, protective clothing is essential to keep the burning sun out, not to keep you warm.

Unlike salmon, bonefish can be greedy feeders. Unlike leaping salmon, bonefish are amazingly camouflaged and difficult to see. Unlike fishing for salmon, you only cast at a 'sighted' fish that is feeding confidently. Bonefish spook if your cast is not perfect.

AND MORE!

Bonefish are not the only fly fisher's quarry in tropical seas. If you want to catch giant fish there are tarpon, tuna, giant trevally and others. Many experts believe that landing an angry, 'lit-up' 45-kg sailfish way offshore is the ultimate fly fishing achievement. They are wrong.

Fly fishing is a journey, not a destination. Each step on the way simply adds new skills and satisfaction. Trout fishers see rivers and lakes as vibrant, living places. They learn to unlock its secrets just as our forefathers did, generations ago, when they had to catch a trout or go hungry. Salt-water fly fishers learn to see bonefish that are invisible to others. They learn to cast with delicacy and precision.

What do salmon fly fishers learn? Hopefully, they learn the most valuable fishing skills of all: persistence and opportunism. They learn to keep going when all seems hopeless. They experiment with new tactics. They also learn that, when conditions are good and salmon are 'vulnerable', they must take full advantage. The window of opportunity will be short.

Do likewise. Enjoy the journey.

APPENDIX ONE

LICENSING BODIES, AGENTS AND OUTFITTERS, SHOPS AND STORES AND OTHERS

LICENSING BODIES

USA
Alaska
www.adfg.alaska.gov

Washington State
www.wdfa.wa.gov/fishing/salmon

Oregon State
www.dfw.state.or.us/resources/fishing/salmon

Canada
British Columbia
www.env.gov.bc.ca/fw/fish

New Brunswick
www.tourismnewbrunswick.ca/Do/fishing

Newfoundland and Labrador
Newfoundland Department of Fisheries and Ocean
(www.nfl.dfo-mpo.gc.ca)

Nova Scotia
www.novascotia.ca/fish

UK
Northern Ireland
www.dcalni.gov.uk

England and Wales
www.gov.uk/fishing-licences

AGENTS AND OUTFITTERS
Fish Pal
(www.fishpal.com)

Frontiers
(www.frontierstrvl.co.uk or www.frontierstravel.com)

The Fly Fishers Group
(www.flyfishergroup.com)

Alaskan Wilderness Safaris
(www.rodgunresources.com).

Go Fishing
(www.gofishingworldwide.co.uk)

World Sport Fishing
(www.worldsportfishing.com)

Roxtons
(www.roxtons.com)

SELECTED FISHERIES, ASSOCIATIONS AND ACCOMMODATION

Alaska
Nakalilok Bay Camp with Alaskan Wilderness Safaris
www.rodgunresources.com

Canada
Newfoundland
Grey River Lodge
(www.flyfishinggreyriver.com)

Scotland
Gualin Estate – Dionard Loch and river fishing
(www.gualin-estate.com)

River Lochy Association
(www.riverlochy.co.uk).

'Big house' accommodation in Scotland
Camisky Lodge
(www.camiskylodge.co.uk)

Scottish fishing clubs with salmon fishing
Forres Angling Association
(www.spanglefish.com/forresanglingassociation)

Inverness Angling Club
(www.invernessanglingclub.co.uk)

Grantown-on-Spey Angling Club
(www.speyfishing-grantown.co.uk)

England and Wales

Hotels with private salmon fishing
Arundell Arms, Lifton, Devon
(www.arundellarms.com)

Riverdale Hall, Bellingham, Northumberland
(www.riverdalehallhotel.co.uk)

Helpful website
www.fishing.visitwales.com)

Ireland

Fisheries
Delphi Lodge
(www.delphilodge.ie)

Hotels with private salmon fishing
Ballynahinch Castle
(www.ballynahinch-castle.com)

Helpful website
(www.fishinginireland.info)

Fishing clubs with salmon fishing
Bangor Erris Angling Club
(www.bangorerrisangling.com)

Norway

Fishery
Gaula Fly Fishing Friends (GFF)
(www.gaulaflyfishing.no)

Helpful website
www.visitnorway.com/fishing-in-norway

Russia

Fisheries
Ponoi River Company
(www.ponoiriver.com)

Atlantic Salmon Reserve (ASR)
(www.kharlovka.com)

SHOPS AND STORES

UK
Belfast Angling Centre,
Argyle Business Centre,
North Howard Street,
Belfast
BT13 2AU
Tel. 028 9031 3156
www.fishingtackle2u.co.uk

Farlows,
9 Pall Mall,
London
SW1Y 5NP
Tel. 020 748 410000

Glasgow Angling Centre,
Unit 1, The Point Retail Park,
29 Saracen Street,
Glasgow
G22 5HT
Tel. 0871 716 1670
www.fishingmegastore.com

John Norris of Penrith,
21 Victoria Road,
Penrith,
Cumbria, CA11 8HP
Tel. 01768 864211
www.johnnorris.co.uk

Sportfish,
Winforton,
Hereford, HR3 6SP
Tel. 01544 327111

Haywards Farm,
Theale,
Reading, RG7 4AS
Tel. 01189 303860
www.sportfish.co.uk

Weir Wood Angling Ltd,
Weir Wood Fishing Lodge,
Weir Wood Reservoir,
Priory Lane, Forest Row,
Sussex, RH18 5HT
Tel. 01342 820650
www.weirwoodangling.co.uk

USA
Cabela's – The world's foremost outfitter
(www.cabelas.com)

FISHING TACKLE MAKERS/SUPPLIERS
www.airflofishing.com
www.greysfishing.com
www.orvis.co.uk
www.snowbee.co.uk
www.tightlines.co.uk

LEAD BODY FOR ANGLING

UK (Incorporating the Angling Development Board)
Angling Trust and Fish Legal,
Eastwood House,
6 Rainbow Street,
Leominster,
Herefordshire, HR6 8DQ
Tel. 08447 700616
www.anglingtrust.net

INSTRUCTION FROM LICENSED COACHES

UK
www.gameanglinginstructors.co.uk

USA
www.fedflyfishers.org

MAGAZINES

UK
Trout and Salmon, published by Bauer Consumer Media Ltd
www.greatmagazines.co.uk

Total Flyfisher, published by David Hall Publishing Ltd
www.totalflyfisher.com

Fly Fishing and Fly Tying, published by Rolling River Publications Ltd
www.flyfishing-and-flytying.co.uk

USA
Field and Stream, published by the Bonnier Corporation, USA
www.fieldandstream.com

APPENDIX TWO

THE ESSENTIAL FLY LIST – DRESSINGS

POPULAR IN UK

Red and yellow tube

    Length – one and a half-inch aluminium tube

    Thread – black Veniard 6/0

    Rear body – medium gold mylar (secured with 'invisible' thread)

    Body 'wing' – white buck tail (optional)

    Front body – black Spirit River lite-bright dubbing

    Rib – medium gold oval tinsel

    Wings – separate bunches of yellow and red buck tail

    Head – black varnish or a gold cone head

Overall length approx. two inches

Also tied on size 10 doubles as an autumn fly

Willie Gunn tube

    Length – one and a quarter inch plastic tube

    Thread – black Veniard 6/0

    Body – black floss silk

    Rib – wide gold tinsel

    Wing – yellow, then orange, then black buck tail

    Head – gold cone head

Overall length approx. two inches

Also tied on size 8 and 10 doubles

Orange shrimp

Hook – low water doubles size 8–10
Thread – hot-orange Veniard 6/0
'Tail' – red golden pheasant flank feather (tied like a hackle and smoothed down to form a 'tail')
Rear body – touching turns of medium gold oval tinsel
Body hackle – six turns of hot orange
Front body – black Spirit River lite-bright dubbing
Rib – medium gold oval tinsel
Front hackle – six turns of 'henny' badger cock

Stinchar stoat

Hook – Salar black size 10–14
Thread – black Veniard 6/0
Tail – yellow arctic fox fur
Body – black Spirit River lite-bright dubbing
Rib – medium silver flat tinsel (over-wound with fine silver wire to prevent the tinsel breaking)
Wing – black squirrel tail or similar
Hackle – hot-orange cock
Head – black varnish

Ally's shrimp

Hook – Salar black size 8 and 10
Thread – red Veniard 6/0
Tail – red buck tail 2 x body length
Rear body – red floss silk
Front body – black floss silk
Rib – silver tinsel
Wing – grey squirrel tail
Cheeks – gold pheasant tippets
Hackle – orange
Head – red varnish

FROM ICELAND AND SCANDINAVIA AND USED EVERYWHERE

Red Francis

> Normally tied on a one inch copper tube or size 8 double hook
>
> Thread – black Veniard 6/0
>
> Feelers – 4 brown, 2 white, stripped saddle hackle stems about one and a half-inches long
>
> Tail – bunch of ginger calf's tail
>
> Butt – Red wool tied round thickly
>
> Body hackle – red game four or five turns tied in as a collar in front of butt
>
> Rib – gold tinsel
>
> Front body – tapering, ribbed red wool

Black snaelda

> Normally tied on a one-inch copper tube or size 8 double hook
>
> Feelers – six strands of pearl Krystal Flash
>
> Tail – black squirrel tail
>
> Body hackle – black, tied as a collar at rear of body
>
> Body – black chenille
>
> Rib – silver tinsel
>
> Front hackle – yellow
>
> Head – black

Sunray Shadow Variant

> Length – one and a half-inch aluminium or rigid plastic tube
>
> Thread – Olive 'Kelvar'
>
> Body – pearl mylar (secured with 'invisible' thread)
>
> Under-wing – white DNA Frost Fish Fibre (about two inches)
>
> Over-wing – medium olive Holo Fusion DNA topped with two or three peacock herls (about three inches long)
>
> Eyes – holographic black and silver (secured with Bug Bond or hard-as-nails varnish)
>
> Head (optional) – silver cone head

The 'original' Sunray Shadow uses white buck tail and black arctic fox fur for the wings.

THREE FROM ALASKA

Chartreuse spider web
> Hook – size 2 to 4 single
> Thread – chartreuse
> Tail – green Flashabou and lime Krystal Flash
> Body – chartreuse Cactus chenille
> Hackle – soft, long chartreuse saddle hackle

Purple woolie shrimp
> Hook – size 4 single
> Thread – red
> Tail – hot-pink goat hair, long
> Body – purple chenille
> Hackle – purple saddle hackle palmered over body
> Collar – purple marabou tied in all round the fly to veil the body
> Head – red varnish

Sockeye orange
> Hook – size 2 to 4 single
> Thread – orange
> Tag – flat gold tinsel
> Tail – red squirrel tail
> Body – gold mylar tied flat around hook shank
> Wing – red squirrel tail
> Hackle – orange
> Head – orange chenille around a pair of gold bead eyes

IRISH AND SCOTTISH 'LOCH-STYLE' FLIES

Connemara black

Hook – size 8
Tail – gold pheasant crest
Body – black seal fur
Rib – fine oval silver tinsel
Hackle – black cock hackle, with blue feather from a jay's wing in front
Wings – bronze mallard flank

Curry's red shrimp

Hook – size 8 or 6
Thread – 6/0 red
Tag – flat silver tinsel
Tail – golden pheasant red flank feather
Rear body – red seal fur ribbed with medium oval tinsel
Mid-hackle – badger
Front body – black seal fur ribbed with medium oval tinsel
Wings – jungle cock
Front hackle – badger
Head – red varnish

Clan chief muddler

Hook – size 8 or 6
Thread – 6/0 black
Tail – red over yellow wool
Body – black seal fur ribbed with fine silver wire
Hackle – red and black cock wound together, tied palmer
  Style
Head – 'spun', trimmed deer hair 'muddler' style

GLOSSARY

American fishing tackle manufacturers (AFTM) rating – this is a worldwide standard by which the tensile strength of fly rods and the weight of the fly lines they cast is determined. It means that no matter where in the world you buy a fly rod or a fly line, a #7 weight-rated rod is designed to cast a #7 weight-rated fly line. Rods and line vary from an ultra-lightweight #1 weight to #14 weights designed to cast heavy flies at, and to land, oceanic giants such as marlin.

Artificials – generic name for all artificial flies.

Bass – a proprietary bag or sack designed to keep newly caught fish fresh. There are many types on the market.

Beat – a stretch of river owned for salmon sport fishing. Usually rented by its owner to tenants for a short period, typically a week in Scotland.

Bomber – a floating salmon fly tied using 'spun' deer hair.

Bugs – small, highly weighted lures used for catching visible fish in clear water fisheries, sometimes in quite deep water.

Chenille – a velvet thread used to tie fly and lure bodies. 'Fritz' Chenille has especially long, fluorescent strands.

Croy – a natural or artificial outcrop in a pool that alters the current and creates 'lies' for salmon.

Double haul – a casting technique using a single-handed rod to increase distance.

Dropper – a 20-cm spur of nylon to which an 'extra' fly can be attached to a leader. The 'spur' is made by tying a three- or four-turn water knot in a leader

Dry flies – flies designed to float on the surface of the water. They are usually tied using stiff neck hackles that ride on the surface film from specially bred cockerels.

Dubbed – the use of a waxed thread onto which fur is twisted to form the body of an artificial fly.

Fly – any hook dressed with feathers, fur or synthetic materials, no matter whether it imitates an insect or not is known as a fly as long as it is light enough to be cast by a fly rod and fly line. It must not incorporate any edible bait.

Fly line – a thick, plastic-coated line which is usually tapered and which provides the weight to cast an almost weightless fly on a short, fine leader. Fly lines are designed to sink or to float. Sinking lines are graded to sink at different speeds. Different manufacturers have a range of specifications for their sinking lines.

Fly pattern – the recipe of materials that make a specific fly is the pattern. Some fly patterns have been recorded for over one hundred years.

Fly reel – a reel designed with a spool to accommodate a fly line and to be used on a fly rod.

Fly rod – a flexible rod designed to cast a heavy fly line and an almost weightless artificial fly.

Fresh salmon – a fish that has only recently entered fresh water and retains its oceanic silver colour.

Gold head – a fly pattern which incorporates a gold bead.

Grilse – a small Atlantic Salmon that has returned to the river to breed after only one winter at sea.

Induced take – moving a fly that is close to a visible salmon or trout to encourage it to grab it.

Intermediate fly line – a very slow-sinking fly line.

Landing Net – a net with a handle used to lift a hooked fish from the water.

Leader – the length of fine nylon monofilament or fluorocarbon line tied onto the fly line to which a tippet and fly are tied. Beginners are advised to use tapered leaders to aid casting.

Lie – an area, which can be large or small, in a pool or stream where salmon rest either temporarily or semi-permanently before moving on upstream.

Marabou – fluffy feathers used in many lure patterns to give mobility to the finished fly.

Mending the line – using the rod to lift a floating fly line off the water and flick it upstream or downstream to adjust the position of the line i.e. to slow down or speed up the movement of the line and fly in the current.

Osenka salmon – these are fish found in some Russian rivers that run into the river in late summer, remain under the ice when the rivers freeze over during the winter and eventually breed the following autumn.

Priest – a short cosh-like tool used to kill fish. There are many designs on the market.

Pull – another word for a take.

Red Game and **Cree** – popular colours of hackle feathers used to tie flies

Retrieving – using the free hand to pull the fly line through the rod rings after casting so that the fly on the end of the leader moves through the water back towards the fisher. The retrieved line is allowed to fall at their feet.

Rise – an individual salmon visibly breaking the water surface.

Rise, Take or **Pull** – when a fish engulfs an artificial fly and this is either seen or felt by the angler.

Shooting or running line – a thin line attached to, or part of, a shooting head or weight forward line which helps long casts by reducing friction as it passes through the rod rings.

Skagit line – a specially designed WF fly line matched to a Switch rod which aids Spey casting.

Spey cast – a form of roll cast using a double-handed fly rod that is used when there is insufficient space behind for a standard over-head cast.

Springer – an Atlantic Salmon that runs into its native river in spring usually after two winters at sea.

Stale salmon – a fish that has been in the river for some time and is displaying its breeding colours and condition.

Take – the pull on the line felt when a salmon takes your fly.

Tippet – a short length of fine line to which the fly is attached, usually on the end of a tapered, nylon monofilament leader.

Weighted Fly – a fly which incorporates extra weight (usually lead wire) to make it sink more quickly.

Wet flies – flies that are designed to be fished below the surface of the water. They are traditionally tied using natural fur and softer neck feathers (hackles) that sink easily through the surface film.

Wide-arbour – a feature of modern fly reels to increase the spool diameter and reduce tight coil memory in fly lines.

Weight Forward (WF) fly line – fly lines are made with different tapers and profiles. A weight forward line has its weight concentrated into its first ten metres or so. This tapered head is followed by a much finer running line to help the line 'shoot' a long way when it is cast.

BIBLIOGRAPHY

Ashley-Cooper, John – *A Salmon Fisher's Odyssey*, published by Witherby.

Buller, Fred – *The Doomsday Book of Giant Salmon*, published by Constable & Robinson.

Falkus, Hugh – *Salmon Fishing*, published by Witherby.

Kelson, George M. – *The Salmon Fly. How to Tie it and How to Use It*, published by Kessinger Publishing.

MacKenzie, Gregor – *Memoirs of a Ghillie*, published by David and Charles.

Owen, Peter – *The Pocket Guide to Fishing Knots*, published by Merlin Unwin Books.

Scott, Jock – *Greased Line Fishing for Salmon*, published by André Deutsch.

Spencer, Sidney – *Salmon and Sea Trout in Wild Places*, published by Witherby.

Spencer, Sidney – *Game Fishing Tactics*, published by Witherby.

Symonds, John and Philip Maher – *Fly Casting Skills for Beginner and Expert*, published by Merlin Unwin Books.

INDEX

Fly fishing for salmon